P9-CFE-274

# LEARN TO
# crochet

# LEARN TO
# crochet

EDITED BY **Sally Harding**

PHOTOGRAPHS BY
**John Heseltine**

Sterling Publishing Co., Inc.
New York

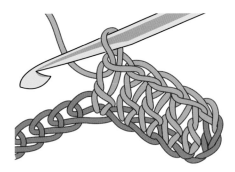

*Editor*  Sally Harding
*Design*  Anne Wilson
*Illustrations*  Kate Simunek
*Photography*  John Heseltine
*Styling*  Susan Berry

Library of Congress Cataloging-in-
Publication Data Available

10  9  8  7  6  5  4  3  2  1

Published by Sterling Publishing Co., Inc.
387 Park Avenue South, New York, NY 10016
Copyright © 2005 Coats Crafts UK
Distributed in Canada by Sterling Publishing
c/o Canadian Manda Group, 165 Dufferin
Street, Toronto, Ontario, Canada M6K 3H6

*Printed in Singapore*
*All rights reserved*

Sterling ISBN 1-4027-2869-7

For information about custom editions,
special sales, premium and corporate
purchases, please contact Sterling Special
Sales Department at 800-805-5489 or
specialsales@sterlingpub.com.

# Contents

# Introduction

Crochet can be used for a wide variety of fabric textures, ranging from a dense, hard-wearing one to a delicate lacy one, depending on the hook size and yarn weight chosen. It is surprisingly quick to create, particularly when using larger hooks and thicker yarns. It has many uses, including acting as an excellent finishing device for knitting garments: joining seams, for example, or creating a neat edging on a sleeve or neck opening. A few sample edgings are shown on pages 26–27, but there are many different ones to choose from.

Although out of fashion for some years, crochet is again very popular, and is being used increasingly by today's up-and-coming textile designers. Its return has heralded a range of interesting household soft furnishings, such as cushion covers and throws, as well as great variety of accessories, such as hats, bags, and scarves. Crochet is ideally suited to these items, as it is quick to work and there are some great, but simple, textural stitches.

This book explains the basics of crochet in a comprehensive, clearly illustrated step-by-step section. Crochet is simple to learn, but the dexterity needed to manipulate the hook and yarn does take a little practice, so try making some small stitch samples in the principal stitches, single, half double, and double crochet, to make sure you can work easily and evenly. After that you can pick out designs form the gallery of projects, from the very simplest, such as a scarf, to more complex patterns, such as the lacy cushion, which require more skill. As guidance for which projects to tackle if you are a beginner, each project is marked with asterisks to indicate complexity: one asterisk indicates a simple project, two an intermediate project, and three an advanced project. Beginners would be advised to start with the easiest and work their way through to the more advanced ones.

Many of the projects in this book are worked as straight pieces of crochet, but if you wish to work "in the round," which involves increasing the stitches in the "rounds" to make circular items, follow the instructions in the relevant patterns (see also, page 22).

Equally, you can create an interesting mesh fabric, known as filet crochet. It is relatively easy and quick to work, and is great for producing figurative images since, like cross stitch, it is based on a system of squares making it is easy to design your own geometric filet crochet motifs.

A simple scallop pattern is easy to work and makes a great texture for a cushion cover (see pages 54–55). A similar pattern can be used to create attractive edgings (see pages 26–27).

# Yarns and threads

There is a wide range of crochet yarns available. Special crochet cottons are the easiest to work with, but you could also use string, wire, or even leather, if you wish. Traditional fine mercerized cotton crochet thread is still widely used for delicate crochet work. It washes beautifully and never loses its color or elasticity. A number of different thickness are produced in this type of thread—the finest is No. 100 and the thickest is No. 5. The popular No. 10 and No. 20 are available in the widest range of colors.

Generally, the fine crochet threads are used for lace-like crochet, such as the filet cushion on pages 68–69, the lacy cushion on page 62–65, and the Christmas decorations on pages 72–77.

For a thicker, more solid crochet fabric, you can use the lightweight, medium-weight, and heavyweight cotton and wool yarns made for both crochet and knitting. These are ideal for crocheted afghans (see pages 58–61) and for cushion covers (see pages 34–41).

Here are the different types and weights of yarns used in this book. At the top are wool yarns in light and medium weights. Below left, center, and right are the special crochet yarns in typical weights and textures, and bottom right are skeins of pearl cotton embroidery thread, which comes in a vast range of colors and is suitable for small projects (see coin purse on pages 52–53).

# Hook types and sizes

There is a wide range of crochet hook sizes to choose from, and the hooks are made in different materials. Formerly only steel or plastic hooks were available, but there is now a range of bamboo hooks, right, which are great to work with—they feel good in the hand and the yarn slides on and off smoothly. They look more attractive, too!

The choice of hook size is determined both by the yarn used in the project you are working on and the degree of laciness of the stitch. The table opposite gives all the hook sizes and shows how the different hook-sizing systems compare.

The larger the hook and the thicker the yarn, the quicker your work will grow.

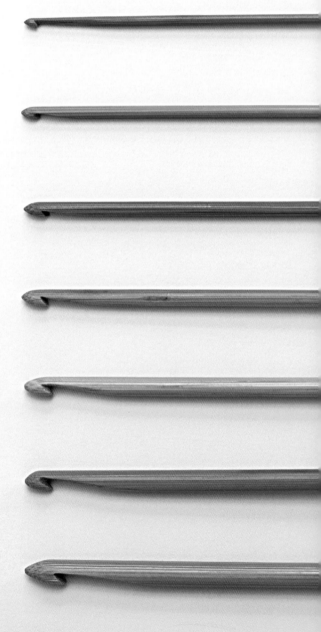

A selection of bamboo crochet hooks in popularly used sizes. The finest are generally used for lace-like crochet, the thicker ones for working with thicker cotton and wool crochet and knitting yarns.

## Crochet hooks sizes

The crochet hook sizes quoted in the instructions in this book are US sizes (with metric sizes in parentheses). Different countries have different hook-sizing systems.

The conversion chart below shows how the various hook sizings relate to each other, although in many cases the conversions do not match exactly. Metric sizing is easy to understand as it indicates the diameter of the hook.

**HOOK CONVERSION CHART**

| US sizes | old UK | EU Metric |
|---|---|---|
| 14 steel | | .60mm |
| 12 steel | | .75mm |
| 11 steel | | 1.00mm |
| 7 steel | | 1.25mm |
| 6 steel | | 1.50mm |
| 5 steel | | 1.75mm |
| | 14 | 2.00mm |
| B-1 (2.25mm) | | |
| | 12 | 2.50mm |
| C-2 (2.75mm) | | |
| | 10 | 3.00mm |
| D-3 (3.25mm) | | |
| E-4 | 9 | 3.50mm |
| F-5 (3.75mm) | | |
| G-6 | 8 | 4.00mm |
| 7 | 7 | 4.50mm |
| H-8 | 6 | 5.00mm |
| I-9 | 5 | 5.50mm |
| J-10 | 4 | 6.00mm |
| K-10½ | 3 | 6.50mm |
| | 2 | 7.00mm |
| L-11 | | 8.00mm |
| M | | 9.00mm |
| N-13 | | 10.00mm |
| O/P-15 | | 12.00mm |
| Q | | 15.00mm |
| S | | 20.00mm |

## Other materials and equipment

You can add buttons, beads, cords, fringes, and tassels to finish off crochet projects.

It helps to give a professional look to projects if you add smart finishing touches. Scarves look good with fringes, either beaded (see page 46) or twisted (see page 57), and bags can be enhanced with the addition of beaded straps (see page 43).

There is a wide range of bead sizes, colors, and types to choose from, but you may have difficulty threading the finer beads onto crochet yarn. If so, you need to first thread a needle with ordinary sewing thread, then loop the crochet yarn through it to draw it through the bead.

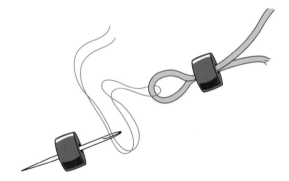

If your yarn is too thick for beads, you can make a simple twisted fringe instead (see page 56).

## Pattern information

The patterns in this book are graded by skill level—easy (✪), intermediate (✪✪), and advanced (✪✪✪). Novices should select the easiest and move to the next level after making a couple of simple projects.

The abbreviations used in these patterns are given on page 21.

# Holding crochet hook

You can hold the hook in various ways, but one of the simplest and easiest methods is to hold the hook like you would a pencil, with the central shaft of the hook gripped between your thumb and index finger as shown. If you prefer, you can hold the hook in the palm of your hand, between your thumb and first two fingers, like a knife.

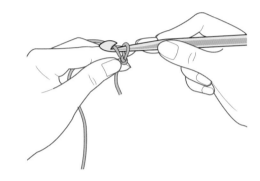

When working crochet, remember to hold the base of the crochet with the first two fingers of the hand holding the yarn, as shown. This allows you to create some tension on the yarn, which is essential when pulling the hook and looped yarn through the previously made stitch.

# Holding yarn

You will need to be able to control the flow of yarn consistently and evenly from the ball of working yarn. One way to do this is to thread the yarn through the fingers of the left hand (if you are right-handed) as shown, with a single twist around the little finger, and with the yarn then running behind the fourth and third fingers, and over the index finger, as shown. However, most crocheters tend to find their own working method.

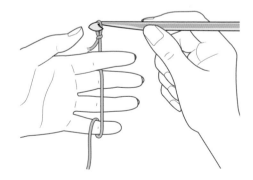

# Making a loop

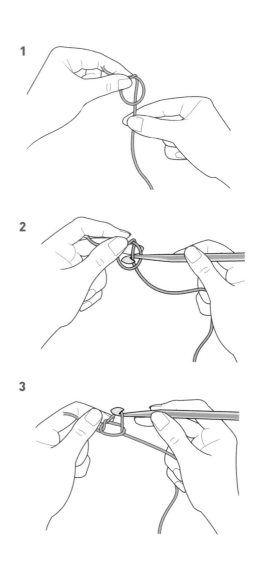

To start to crochet you need to create a first loop on the hook. There are various methods of doing this, but the one shown here is easy and quick.

**1** Grasp the end of the yarn between your thumb and index finger. Form the yarn into a loop, held in place between the thumb and the index finger, and position the ball end of the yarn behind the loop.

**2** Holding the hook like a pencil, insert it through the center of the loop and catch the yarn strand behind the loop with the crochet hook.

**3** Draw the yarn through the loop to create a loop around the hook.

**4** Pull the tail end of the yarn in the opposite direction to tighten the new loop around the hook. Do not pull the yarn too tight. The loop should slide easily on the hook.

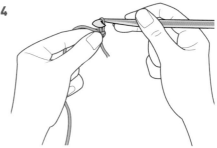

# Foundation chain

To "cast on" in crochet you will need to make a foundation chain. After you have made your first loop on the crochet hook, you then continue to make stitches as follows.

**1** Catch the tail end of the yarn between your thumb and index finger and hold it firmly.

**2** Catch the ball end of the yarn with the hook, by passing the hook over and under the yarn in a twisting motion as shown by the arrow.

**3** Draw the yarn now wrapped around the hook through the loop on the hook to make a chain (abbreviated in patterns as ch). Remember to hold on to the end of the chains with your other hand, to create sufficient tension as you make the stitches. Continue in this way until the required number of chains has been made (known in crochet patterns as the foundation chain).

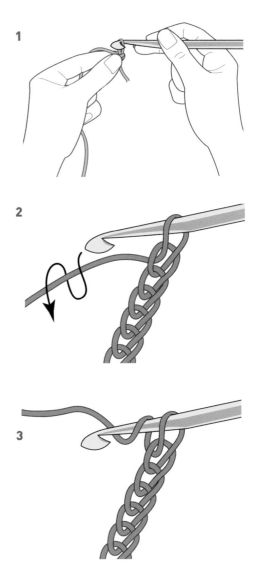

# Basic stitches

## Slip stitch

The shortest and easiest of the basic crochet stitches is slip stitch. On its own it forms a dense fabric, but it is usually used only as an edging or as a joining stitch.

To work a slip stitch on a foundation chain, insert the hook into the SECOND chain from the hook, catch the yarn with the hook (as shown in making a foundation chain) and draw the yarn through the chain and the loop on the hook to complete the stitch.

## Working basic stitches in rows

When you turn your crochet work at the end of a row, in order to start the next row you will need to add a specific number of chain stitches—called "turning chains"—to bring the work into the right position to create the stitches for the next row. The chart below gives the number of turning chains required for the various basic crochet stitches.

The turning chains used for double crochet and taller stitches usually count as the first stitch in the row.

**TURNING CHAINS**
slip stitch—1ch
single crochet—1ch
half double—2ch
double—3ch
treble—4ch
double treble—5ch
triple treble—6ch
quadruple treble—7ch

## Fastening off

To fasten off a piece of crochet when it is complete, first cut the thread about 3in (7cm) from the work. Then pass the loose end through the one remaining loop on the hook, and pull tightly. Darn the loose ends into on the wrong side of the work, using a blunt-ended yarn needle.

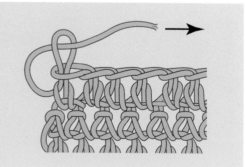

# Single crochet

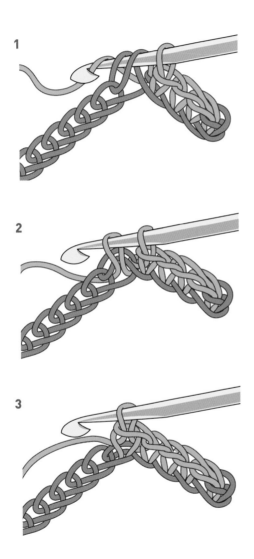

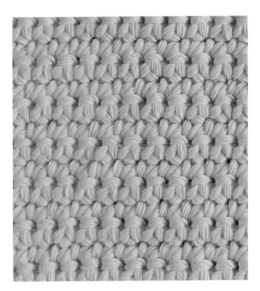

Single crochet is the most commonly used stitch in crochet and is abbreviated in patterns as sc. It creates a dense, hard-wearing textile, ideal for mats, bags, or containers. It is sometimes known as "plain stitch." In fact, the very plain nature of the stitch is also one of its most attractive features.

**How to work single crochet**

**1** Make a foundation chain (see page 14), then insert the hook through the SECOND chain from the hook and catch the yarn with the hook (known as yarn over hook or yo).

**2** Draw the hook through the chain so that there are now two loops on the hook.

**3** Wrap the yarn around the hook and draw it through the two loops on the hook—one loop remains on the hook. Work a single crochet in each chain in the same way. On the following rows, work the one turning chain (see page 15), then work one single crochet in each stitch of the previous row.

# Half doubles

**1**

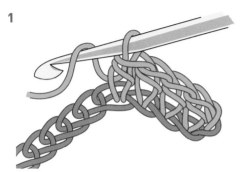

**2**

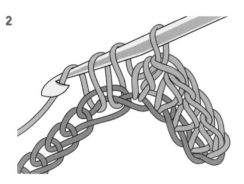

**3**

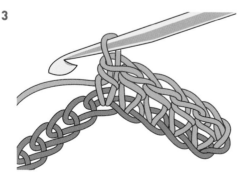

Half double is abbreviated as hdc in patterns. It is made in a similar way to a single crochet but an additional twist of yarn is made around the hook before the stitch is started. This creates a slightly less dense and more flexible fabric than single crochet.

## How to work half doubles

**1** Make a foundation chain, then wrap the yarn around the hook and insert the hook through the THIRD chain from the hook.

**2** Wrap the yarn around the hook and draw it through the chain so that there are now three loops on the hook.

**3** Wrap the yarn around the hook again and draw it through all three loops to complete the stitch. Work a half double in each chain. To start the following rows, first work the two turning chains, then skip the first stitch and work one stitch in each of the remaining stitches of the previous row, working the last stitch in the top of the turning chain.

# Double crochet

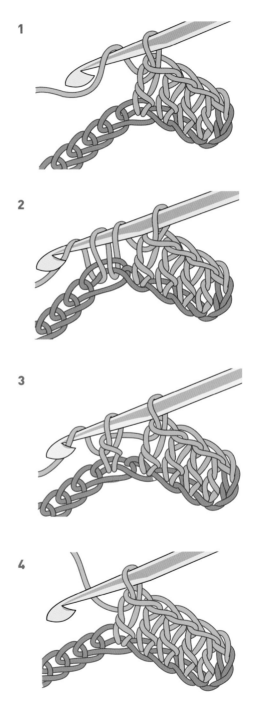

Doubles are taller than half doubles and produce a more airy-looking fabric that is softer than either single or half double crochet. It is often used for lacy garments and household items.

## How to work double crochet

**1** Yo and insert the hook through the FOURTH chain from the hook. Yo and draw the yarn through the chain.

**2** Yo and draw the yarn through the first two loops on the hook.

**3** Yo and draw the yarn through the two remaining loops on the hook.

**4** One loop remains on the hook. Work a double in each chain in the same way. Work the following rows as for half doubles, but make three turning chains.

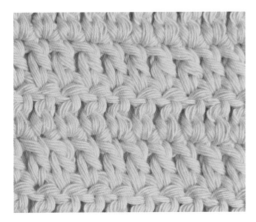

## Treble crochet

This is worked as for double crochet, except that the yarn is wrapped twice around the hook before starting each stitch and four turning chains are used in subsequent rows.

Yo twice and insert the hook in the FIFTH chain from the hook. Yo and draw a loop through the chain—four loops are now on the hook. *Yo and draw through two loops on the hook. Repeat from * twice more—the stitch is completed and one loop remains on the hook. Work a treble in each chain in the same way.

## Double trebles

In this stitch (and the taller triple and quadruple trebles), the stitch is begun with three (or four or five) yarn wraps, and the loops are worked off the hook two at a time until one loops remains, in exactly the same way as for doubles and trebles. A stitch is worked in each chain, then on the subsequent rows a turning chain is worked to count as the first stitch of the row (see page 15).

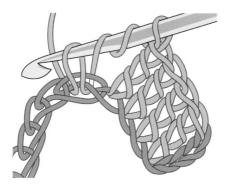

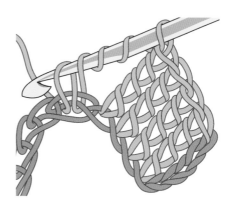

# Gauge

To ensure that you are working to the right measurements, and that the finished project will be the required size, you need to check the gauge of the fabric you create against the gauge given at the beginning of each pattern. This is indicated as rows and stitches over a 4in (10cm) block of crochet worked in the main pattern stitch of the project.

To check your gauge, crochet a 5in (13cm) sample using the hook size and yarn specified, and then measure the rows and stitches as shown below.

If your gauge is too loose (fewer stitches and rows than that specified), use a finer hook. If it is too tight (more stitches and rows than that of the pattern), use a larger hook.

For some projects the final size is not particularly important: when making a blanket, for example. In this case, obtaining the correct gauge is not critical. However, if you wish to ensure that a cushion cover is the right size for an existing pillow form, for example, you will need to work to the correct gauge (as you do if making fitted crochet garments).

The gauge square shown right is worked in double crochet in a lightweight cotton yarn. When measuring your gauge, mark out 4in (10cm) on the sample and measure the number of rows (vertically) and the number of stitches (horizontally).

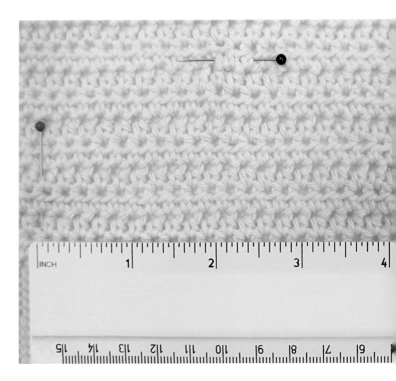

# Working from patterns

## Crochet abbreviations

Here are the standard abbreviations used for US crochet patterns. Most of them are used in the patterns in this book and others are here in case you come across them in other books.

### ABBREVIATIONS FOR CROCHET STITCHES

| | |
|---|---|
| ch | chain(s) |
| dc | double crochet |
| dtr | double treble |
| hdc | half double |
| qtr | quadruple treble |
| sc | single crochet |
| sl st | slip stitch |
| tr | treble |
| trtr | triple treble |

### GENERAL CROCHET ABBREVIATIONS

| | |
|---|---|
| alt | alternate |
| approx | approximately |
| beg | begin(ning) |
| blk(s) | block(s) |
| ch-sp | chain space |
| CC | contrasting color |
| cm | centimeter(s) |
| cont | continu(e)(ing) |
| dec | decreas(e)(ing) |
| foll | follow(s)(ing) |
| g | gram(s) |
| in | inch(es) |
| inc | increas(e)(ing) |
| lp(s) | loop(s) |
| m | meter(s) |
| MC | main color |
| mm | millimeter(s) |
| oz | ounce(s) |
| patt(s) | pattern(s) |

| | |
|---|---|
| rem | remain(s)(ing) |
| rep | repeat(s)(ing) |
| rnd(s) | round(s) |
| RS | right side |
| sp(s) | space(s) |
| st(s) | stitch(es) |
| t-ch | turning chain |
| tog | together |
| WS | wrong side |
| yd | yard(s) |
| yo | yarn over hook |

\* Repeat instructions after asterisk or between asterisks as many times as instructed.

[ ] ( ) Repeat instructions inside square brackets or parentheses as many times as instructed.

## Crochet terminology

Crochet terminology is different in the US and UK, so if you buy a book when abroad it is helpful to note the differences. This book is written with US terminology. The UK equivalents are given below:

| US | UK |
|---|---|
| single crochet (sc) | double crochet (dc) |
| half double (hdc) | half treble (htr) |
| double crochet (dc) | treble crochet (tr) |
| triple (tr) | double treble (dtr) |
| double treble (dtr) | triple treble (trtr) |
| triple treble (trtr) | quadruple treble (qtr) |
| quadruple treble (qtr) | quintuple treble (quintr) |
| yarn over hook (yo) | yarn round hook (yrh) |
| skip | miss |
| slip stitch (sl st) | slip stitch (ss) |

# Working in rounds

If you want to create a piece of crochet fabric that is circular, such as a round table mat or the base of a bag, you will have to start with a chain circle. This is created quite simply from a suitable length of foundation chains that are then linked end to end to form a ring.

**1** Make a foundation chain (see page 14) of the appropriate number of chains, in this case six. Insert the hook into the first chain worked and catch the yarn with hook.

**2** Draw the yarn through both the chain and the loop on the hook to join the length of chains into a circle—this is called "join with a slip stitch."

**3** The first "round" of the crochet is worked into the ring. The instructions in your pattern for "round 1" will tell you what stitches and how many to work—here single crochet stitches are being worked into the ring. In the following rounds stitches are increased by working twice into the same stitch where instructed. The work is not turned at the end of rounds, so the right side of the crochet is always facing you.

This little crochet circle is the jug cover on pages 52–53. It is worked in the round, starting from a foundation chain of 6ch, which is joined with a slip stitch to create the ring. The following rounds are worked in doubles, then chain loops with picots.

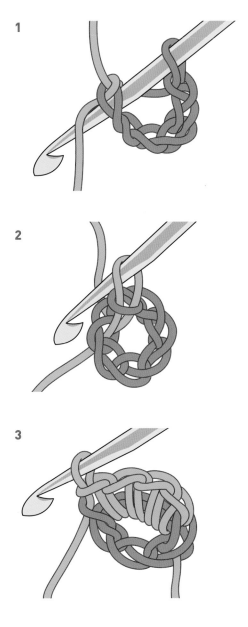

1

2

3

# Working filet crochet

Filet crochet creates an airy texture with
neatly spaced geometric holes (referred to
as spaces); the connecting stitches are
referred to as bars and the filled in spaces
are called blocks.

Filet crochet is ideal for net edgings for
pillows and hand towels, or for geometric-
style projects. Traditionally worked in fine
white cotton, filet crochet can be worked
instead in brightly colored cotton crochet
threads for contemporary-looking projects.

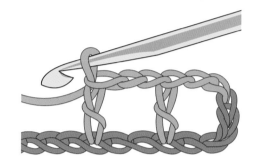

Making spaces

## Making spaces

These are abbreviated as sp or sps.

To make a row of spaces, work 1dc in the
8th ch from the hook, then *ch2, skip 2ch,
work 1dc in next chain. Repeat from * to end
of chain.

## Block and space

These are referred to in patterns as block
(blk) and space (sp).

Work 1dc in 4th chain from hook, 1dc into
each of next 2ch, *ch2, skip 2ch, 1dc in each
of next 4ch. Repeat from *.

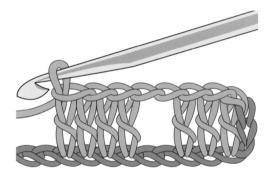

Block and space

## Bar and lacet

Bars and lacets are sometimes used in
combination with basic filet patterns.

To make a bar, ch5, skip 5 stitches or a
lacet, 1dc in next stitch. To make a lacet, ch3,
skip 2 stitches, 1sc in next stitch, ch3, skip 2
stitches, 1dc in next stitch.

Bar and lacet

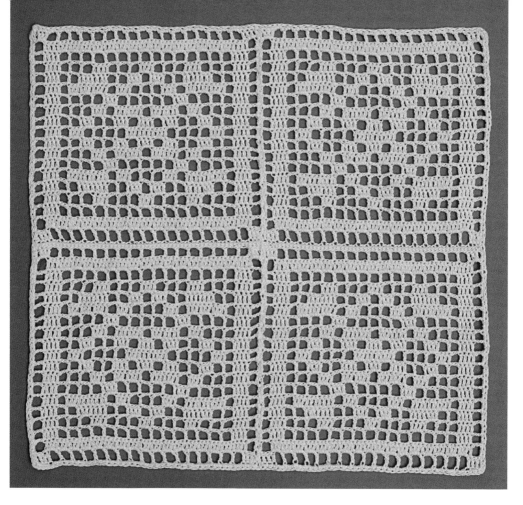

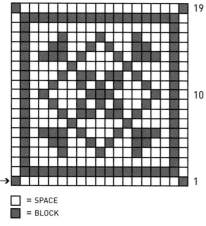

19

10

1

→

□ = SPACE
■ = BLOCK

Four individual filet squares are stitched together to form the center decoration for the crochet cushion on pages 68–69.

## Filet pillow chart

Instructions for filet crochet usually start with an explanation of how to make "spaces" and "blocks" and written instructions for the first few rows. Then a chart, similar to the chart here for the Filet Pillow on page 68, is followed with ease for the remaining rows.

# Simple crochet edgings

You can use the edgings shown here for pillows, towels, cushions, collars, and cuffs, for example. All these edgings are made on a foundation chain slightly longer than the desired length of the edging, except for the Fan Edging. You can use fine crochet threads for them, as on towel and pillow edgings on pages 66–67 and 70–71, or a lightweight cotton yarn, as used here for these samples, for garments.

If you like, you can make a sample swatch of your edging first to work out precisely how many chain stitches to start with.

After finishing any edgings, pin out and press them lightly, then stitch to the crocheted, knitted, or fabric item.

## To make loop edging

To begin, make a foundation chain slightly longer than the desired length of the edging. The number of chains must be a multiple of 4, plus 2 extra.

**Row 1 (WS)** 1sc in 2nd ch from hook, 1sc in each of rem ch. Turn.

**Row 2 (RS)** Ch3, skip first 2sc, 1dc in next sc, ch5, *1dc in same sc as last dc, (skip next sc, 1dc in next sc) twice, ch5; rep from * to last 2sc, 1dc in same sc as last dc, skip next sc, 1dc in last sc.
Fasten off.

## To make scallop edging

To begin, make a foundation chain slightly longer than the desired length of the edging. The number of chains must be a multiple of 6, plus 2 extra.

**Row 1 (WS)** 1sc in 2nd ch from hook, 1sc in each of rem ch. Turn.

**Row 2 (RS)** Ch1, 1sc in first sc, *skip next 2sc, 7tr in next sc, skip next 2sc, 1sc in next sc; rep from * to end.
Fasten off.

## To make cluster edging

To begin, make a foundation chain slightly longer than the desired length of the edging. The number of chains must be a multiple of 6, plus 2 extra.

**Row 1 (WS)** 1sc in 2nd ch from hook, 1sc in each of rem ch. Turn.

**Row 2 (RS)** Ch4, then leaving last loop of each tr on hook, work 2tr in first sc, yo and draw a loop through all 3 loops on hook (2tr-cluster made), *ch8, 1sc in 3rd ch from hook (picot made), ch5, then leaving last loop of each tr on hook, work 3tr in same sc as last cluster, yo and draw a loop through all 4 loops on hook (3tr-cluster made), skip next 5sc, 3tr-cluster in next sc; rep from * to end, omitting 3tr-cluster at end of last rep.
Fasten off.

## To make fan edging

To begin, ch12.

**Row 1 (WS)** 1sc in 8th ch from hook, ch5, skip next 3ch, work (1dc, ch3, 1dc) all in next ch. Turn.

**Row 2 (RS)** Ch3, 9dc in 3ch-sp, 1sc in 5ch-loop, ch5, 1sc in 7ch-loop at end. Turn.

**Row 3** Ch7, 1sc in 5ch-loop, ch5, work (1dc, ch3, 1dc) all in 5th dc (center dc) of 9dc group. Turn.

Rep rows 2 and 3 until edging is desired length, ending with a row 2.
Fasten off.

## To make Venetian edging

To begin, make a foundation chain slightly longer than the desired length of the edging. The number of chains must be a multiple of 5, plus 2 extra.

**Row 1 (WS)** 1sc in 2nd ch from hook, 1sc in each of rem ch. Turn.

**Row 2 (RS)** Ch6, 1dc in first sc, *(skip next sc, 1dc in next sc) twice, ch3, 1dc in next sc; rep from * to end. Turn.

**Row 3** Ch1, work (1sc, ch3, 1sc) all in first 3ch-sp, *ch5, work (1sc, ch3, 1sc) all in next 3ch-sp; rep from *, working last (1sc, ch3, 1sc) all in 6ch-loop at end. Turn.

**Row 4** Ch1, 1sc in first 3ch-loop, *ch4, 1tr in next 5ch-loop, ch4, 1sc in next 3ch-loop; rep from * to end. Turn.

**Row 5** 5sc in first 4ch-loop, *ch5, 5sc in each of next 2 4ch-loops; rep from *, ending with 5sc in last 4ch-loop.
Fasten off.

## To make double-picot edging

To begin, make a foundation chain slightly longer than the desired length of the edging. The number of chains must be a multiple of 7, plus 6 extra.

**Row 1 (RS)** 1sc in 2nd ch from hook, 1sc in each of next 2ch, *ch4 and work 1sc in 4rd ch from hook—called *make picot*—, 1sc in each of next 2ch, turn, ch9, 1sc in 3rd sc before picot, turn, work (5sc, make picot, 3sc, make picot, 5sc) all in 9ch-loop, 1sc in each of next 5ch; rep from * to end, omitting 5sc at end of last rep.
Fasten off.

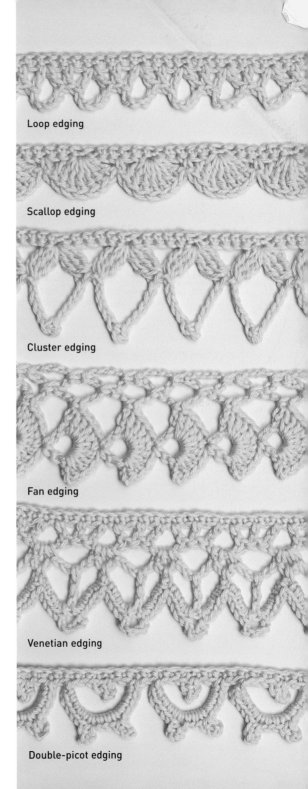

Loop edging

Scallop edging

Cluster edging

Fan edging

Venetian edging

Double-picot edging

# gallery of
# projects

# Single-crochet pot holder

✪ *Crocheted in easy-to-work single crochet, the two layers of this pot holder are joined with a picot edging. Make your own stripes to suit.*

## You will need

- A medium-weight cotton yarn, each ball approx 1³⁄₄oz/76yd (50g/70m):
    - 2 balls in main color (**MC**)—purple
    - 1 ball in contrasting color (**CC**)—orange
- Sizes D-3 (3.00mm), G-6 (4.00mm), and 7 (4.50mm) crochet hooks
- Small metal or plastic ring

## Gauge and finished size

- 17 stitches and 19 rows to 4in (10cm) over sc using size G-6 (4.00mm) hook.
- Pot holder measures 7in (18cm) square, excluding edging.

## To make pot holder

The pot holder has a back and front. The back forms a pocket into which you can slip your hand, or for really hot things you can use the double thickness.

### FRONT

To begin, using size 7 (4.50mm) hook and MC, ch29.

Change to size G-6 (4.00mm) hook and cont.

**Row 1 (RS)** 1sc in 2nd ch from hook, 1sc in each of rem ch. Turn. (28sc)

**Row 2** Ch1, 1sc in first sc, 1sc in each sc to last sc, 1sc in last sc changing to CC with last yo of st. Turn.

Rep row 2 28 times more **and at the same time** work stripe sequence as foll, changing to new color with last yo of previous row:

1 row CC, 7 rows MC, 1 row CC, 9 rows MC, 1 row CC, 5 rows MC, 1 row CC***, 3 rows MC. Fasten off.

### BACK

Work as for front to ***.

Using size D-3 (3.00mm) hook and MC, work one row more in sc.

Fasten off.

### EDGING

**Round 1** Using size D-3 (3.00mm) hook and MC and holding front and back with WS tog and foundation-chain edges aligned, insert hook through edge of both layers of pot holder at center of one side, yo and draw yarn through, ch1, 1sc in same place ch was worked, then work sc evenly around edge of pot holder, working 3sc in each corner and working edging at top through the front only; finish by joining with a sl st in first sc. (Do not turn at end of rounds.)

**Round 2** Ch1, 1sc in same place as sl st, 1sc in each of next 2sc, *ch3, sl st in last sc worked (one picot made), 1sc in each of next 3sc; rep from * around pot holder, but work 3sc in each corner, leave one corner at top free of picots for attaching hanging ring and adjust space between last two picots as necessary to fit; finish by joining with a sl st in first sc. Fasten off.

## To finish

Press. Weave in any loose ends.

Using size D-3 (3.00mm) hook and MC, work sc around ring and join with a sl st to first sc. Fasten off. Stitch to corner of pot holder.

# Simple blanket

✪ *This blanket can be made in two sizes—a baby blanket size and an afghan size. It is worked in single crochet and chain stitches, which creates a soft, supple fabric. Make up your own striped version if you wish.*

## You will need

- A medium-weight cotton yarn, each ball approx 1¾oz/76yd (50g/70m):
    - 12 [**23**] balls in main color (**MC**)—green
    - 2 [**2**] balls in first contrasting color (**A**)—turquoise
    - 1 [**1**] ball in second contrasting color (**B**)—pale blue
    - 1 [**1**] ball in second contrasting color (**C**)—lime
- Sizes I-9 (5.50mm) and J-10 (6.00mm) crochet hooks

## Gauge and finished size

- 20 stitches (10sc and 10 1ch-sps) and 14 rows to 4in (10cm) over pattern stitch using size I-9 (5.50mm) hook.
- Blanket measures 38¾ [**48**]in x 38¾ [**58**]in (97 [**120**]cm x 97 [**148**]cm), including border

## Special note

If desired, you can change the size of the blanket. Figure out how many stitches are needed across the row by using the gauge given above. Make one foundation chain for each stitch needed, plus one extra. If the number of stitches is even, add one more chain to make it an odd number—the pattern requires an odd number of foundation chains.

## To make blanket

To begin, using size J-10 (6.00mm) hook and MC, ch185 [**231**].

Change to size I-9 (5.50mm) hook and cont.

**Row 1** 1sc in 2nd ch from hook, *ch1, skip next ch, 1sc in next ch; rep from * to last ch, 1sc in last ch. Turn.

**Row 2** Ch1, 1sc in first sc, ch1, 1sc in next 1ch-sp; rep from * to last sc, 1sc in last sc. Turn.

Rep row 2 to form patt st until blanket measures 36in (92cm) from beg **and at the same time** work in stripe sequence as foll: 3 rows more in MC, 1 row A, 1 row B, 7 rows MC, 1 row C, 1 row A, 14 rows MC, 1 row C, 22 rows MC, 1 row A, 31 [**101**] rows MC, 1 row A, 1 row B, 3 rows MC, 1 row C, 1 row A, 17 rows MC, 1 row C, 9 rows MC, 1 row C, 1 row A, 8 rows MC.

*Note:* If necessary, stop stripe sequence when blanket measures 36¾ [**46**]in (92 [**115**]cm) from beg (and end with one row MC), or if sequence is complete, cont with MC only until it reaches this length.

Fasten off.

### BORDER

**Round 1** Using size I-9 (5.50mm) hook and MC, insert hook through edge of blanket at any corner, yo and draw yarn through, ch1, 1sc in same place as ch was worked; then work sc evenly around edge of blanket, working 3sc in each corner, and join with a sl st in first sc. (Do not turn at end of rounds but work with same side always facing.)

**Round 2** Ch3, then working into back loop only of sc of previous round, work 1dc in each sc all around edge, except work 3dc in each corner sc, and join with a sl st to 3rd of first 3ch. Fasten off.

**Round 3** Using A (turquoise), insert hook through a dc, yo and draw yarn through, ch1; then working into back loop only of dc of previous round, work 1sc same place as ch was worked and 1sc in each dc all around edge, except work 3sc in each corner dc, and join with a sl st to first sc.

Fasten off.

Weave in any loose ends.

# Circular cushion

✪✪ *You can make this circular cushion with or without its flower motif adornment (see pages 36–37). Make several in different toning colors. It is easy to work once you master the art of working in rounds (see page 22). You could also add a simple picot edging (see pages 26–27) to the cushion in a contrasting color, if you prefer.*

## You will need
- A wool-mix, medium-weight yarn, each ball approx 1³/₄oz/131yd (50g/120m):
  - 3 balls in main color (**MC**)—taupe
  - Small amount in first contrasting color (**A**)—cream
  - Small amount in second contrasting color (**B**)—beige
  - Small amount in third contrasting color (**C**)—terra cotta
- Size G-6 (4.00mm) crochet hook
- Pillow form to fit

## Gauge and finished size
- 18 stitches and 9 rows to 4in (10cm) over double crochet using size G-6 (4.00mm) hook.
- Finished cushion measures approximately 15in (38cm) in diameter.

## To make cushion cover
The cushion cover is made from two identical pieces.

### FRONT AND BACK (BOTH ALIKE)
To begin, using MC ch4 and join with a sl st in first ch to form a ring.

**Round 1 (RS)** Ch3 (3ch at beg of rounds count as first dc), 11dc in ring, 1sl st in 3rd of first 3ch. Do not turn at end of rounds, but work with RS always facing. (12 sts)

**Round 2** Ch3, 1dc in same place as sl st, 2dc in each of rem dc, 1sl st in 3rd of first 3ch. (24 sts)

**Round 3** Ch3, 1dc in same place as sl st, *1dc in next dc, 2dc in each of next 2dc; rep from * to last 2dc, 1dc in next dc, 2dc in last dc, 1sl st in 3rd of first 3ch. (40 sts)

**Round 4** Ch3, 1dc in same place as sl st, *1dc in each of next 3dc, 2dc in next dc; rep from * to last 3dc, 1dc in each of last 3dc, 1sl st in 3rd of first 3ch. (50 sts)

**Round 5** Ch3, 1dc in same place as sl st, *1dc in each of next 4dc, 2dc in next dc; rep from * to last 4dc, 1dc in each of last 4dc, 1sl st in 3rd of first 3ch. (60 sts)

**Round 6** Ch3, 1dc in same place as sl st, *1dc in each of next 5dc, 2dc in next dc; rep from * to last 5dc, 1dc in each of last 5dc, 1sl st in 3rd of first 3ch. (70 sts)

**Round 7** Ch3, 1dc in same place as sl st, *1dc in each of next 6dc, 2dc in next dc; rep from * to last 6dc, 1dc in each of last 6dc, 1sl st in 3rd of first 3ch. (80 sts)

**Round 8** Ch3, 1dc in same place as sl st, *1dc in each of next 7dc, 2dc in next dc; rep from * to last 7dc, 1dc in each of last 7dc, 1sl st in 3rd of first 3ch. (90 sts)

**Round 9** Ch3, 1dc in same place as sl st, *1dc in each of next 8dc, 2dc in next dc; rep from * to last 8dc, 1dc in each of last 8dc, 1sl st in 3rd of first 3ch. (100 sts)

**Round 10** As round 5. (120 sts)

**Round 11** Ch3, 1dc in same place as sl st,

*1dc in each of next 11dc, 2dc in next dc; rep from * to last 11dc, 1dc in each of last 11dc, 1sl st in 3rd of first 3ch. (130 sts)

**Round 12** Ch3, 1dc in same place as sl st, *1dc in each of next 12dc, 2dc in next dc; rep from * to last 12dc, 1dc in each of last 12dc, 1sl st in 3rd of first 3ch. (140 sts)

**Round 13** As round 7. (160 sts)

**Round 14** Ch3, 1dc in same place as sl st, *1dc in each of next 15dc, 2dc in next dc; rep from * to last 15dc, 1dc in each of last 15dc, 1sl st in 3rd of first 3ch. (170 sts)

**Round 15** Ch3, 1dc in same place as sl st, *1dc in each of next 16dc, 2dc in next dc; rep from * to last 16dc, 1dc in each of last 16dc, 1sl st in 3rd of first 3ch. (180 sts)

**Round 16** Ch3, 1dc in same place as sl st, *1dc in each of next 17dc, 2dc in next dc; rep from * to last 17dc, 1dc in each of last 17dc, 1sl st in 3rd of first 3ch. (190 sts)

**Round 17** Ch3, 1dc in same place as sl st, *1dc in each of next 18dc, 2dc in next dc; rep from * to last 18dc, 1dc in each of last 18dc, 1sl st in 3rd of first 3ch. (200 sts)
Fasten off.

**FLOWER MOTIF**

To begin, using B ch4 and join with a sl st in first ch to form a ring.

**Round 1 (RS)** 6sc in ring. Do not turn at end of rounds, but work with RS always facing.

**Round 2** 2sc in each sc. (12 sts)

Then working into back loop only of each sc, cont in a spiral as foll:
(2sc in next sc, 1sc in next sc) 15 times, (2sc in next sc, 1sc in each of next 2sc) 9 times, (2sc in next sc, 1sc in each of next 3sc) 10 times, 1sc in next sc.
Fasten off.

Starting in first unworked front loop of sc near center of flower, add petals as foll:
Using A, (1sl st in next sc, 2dc in each of next 3sc, 1sl st in next sc) 6 times.

Using B, (1sl st in next sc, 2dc in each of next 3sc, 1sl st in next sc) 6 times.
Using C, (1sl st in next sc, 2dc in each of next 3sc, 1sl st in next sc) 17 times.
Fasten off.

**To finish**

Press the front and back of the cushion lightly on WS with a warm iron following the pressing instructions on the yarn label.
Sew flower motif to center of front.

**EDGING**

Place pillow form between back and front and join front and back by working sc around the edge through both layers, using MC.
Fasten off.

Adding one crocheted flower to the center of the front of the cushion adds an interesting detail. The flower motif is worked round and round in a spiral and is great fun to make.

# Striped cushions

✪ *You have an alternative design for this simple blocks and stripes cushion. The version shown opposite is the main pattern, but a simpler version is given on page 40. You can, if you wish, make the cushion front in one pattern and the reverse in the other.*

*You could adapt the design to make a simple throw, too, increasing the quantities of yarn proportionately and picking your own colorways to suit your decor.*

## You will need
- A wool-mix, medium-weight yarn, each ball approx 1³/₄oz/131yd (50g/120m), in following amounts for one cushion:
    - 4 balls in **A**—steel gray
    - 4 balls in **B**—white
- Size G-6 (4.00mm) crochet hook
- Pillow form to fit

## Gauge and finished size
- 19 stitches and 14 rows to 4in (10cm) over striped pattern stitch using size G-6 (4.00mm) hook.
- Each version of the finished cushion measures 18¹/₄in (46cm) square.

## Special note
When changing colors for stripes, change to new color with last yo of last sc of previous row.

## To make strips version
The front and back of the cushion are each made from four strips. Keep track of which strip is which so they can be joined in the correct sequence when complete (pin the strip number to each piece).

**STRIP 1 (MAKE 2)**
To begin, using A ch24.
Beg patt as foll:
**Row 1 (RS)** 1dc in 4th ch from hook, 1dc in each of rem ch. Turn.
**Row 2** Ch1, 1sc in each dc, 1sc in 3rd of 3ch. Turn. (22sc)
**Row 3** Ch3 to count as first dc, skip first sc, *1dc in next sc; rep from * to end.
**Row 4** Ch1, 1sc in each dc, 1sc in 3rd of 3ch. Turn.
Rep rows 3–4 to form patt st.
Cont in patt (of one row dc and one row sc alternately) **and at the same time** work in stripes as foll:
12 more rows A, (2 rows B, 2 rows A) 4 times, 16 rows B, (2 rows A, 2 rows B) 4 times.
Fasten off.

**STRIP 2 (MAKE 2)**
Work as for Strip 1, but in stripe sequence as foll:
(2 rows A, 2 rows B) 4 times times, 16 rows A, (2 rows B, 2 rows A) 4 times, 16 rows B.
Fasten off.

**STRIP 3 (MAKE 2)**
Work as for Strip 1, but in stripe sequence as foll:
16 rows B, (2 rows A, 2 rows B) 4 times, 16 rows A, (2 rows B, 2 rows A) 4 times.
Fasten off.

**STRIP 4 (MAKE 2)**
Work as for Strip 1, but in stripe sequence as foll:
(2 rows B, 2 rows A) 4 times, 16 rows B,

(2 rows A, 2 rows B) 4 times, 16 rows A.
Fasten off.

## To finish
Press the strips lightly on WS following the pressing instructions on the yarn label.
For the cushion front, arrange the strips (with foundation-chain edges aligned) from left to right as foll:
One Strip 1, one Strip 2, one Strip 3, and one Strip 4.
Join strips in this order with a fine backstitch.
For the cushion back, arrange the strips (with foundation-chain edges aligned) from left to right as foll:
One Strip 3, one Strip 4, one Strip 1, and one Strip 2.
Join strips in this order as for front.
Press seams lightly. With right sides together, join front to back around three sides. Turn right side out and insert pillow form. Join opening.

## To make simple stripes version
The cushion cover is made from two identical pieces.
### FRONT AND BACK (BOTH ALIKE)
To begin, using A ch90.
Beg patt as foll:
**Row 1 (RS)** Using A, 1dc in 4th ch from hook, 1dc in each of rem ch. Turn.
**Row 2** Using A, ch1, 1sc in each dc, 1sc in 3rd of 3ch, changing to B with last yo of last sc. Turn. (88sc)
**Row 3** Using B, ch3 to count as first dc, skip first sc, *1dc in next sc; rep from * to end.
**Row 4** Using B, ch1, 1sc in each dc, 1sc in 3rd of 3ch, changing to A with last yo of last sc. Turn.
Rep rows 3–4 to form patt st.
Cont in patt (of one row dc and one row sc

alternately) **and at the same time** work in stripes as foll:
(2 rows A, 2 rows B) 3 times times, 16 rows A, (2 rows B, 2 rows A) 4 times, 16 rows B.
Fasten off.

## To finish
Press the front and back lightly on WS following the pressing instructions on the yarn label.
With right sides together, join front to back around three sides. Turn right side out and insert pillow form. Join opening.

The simple stripes version of the cushion cover is much quicker to work, with just one piece for the front and one piece for the back. You could work a double-crochet back in a single bright contrasting color for an even faster project.

# Colorwork bags

⭐ *Here are two styles of bag with the same basic stitch pattern. The rectangular bag (right) has a beaded chain strap, and the square bag (see page 44) has a crocheted handle.*

*The bags use only single and double crochet stitches, and the bicolor design is not difficult. You could adapt the pattern to make a little coin purse to match (which will take proportionately less yarn).*

## You will need

### SQUARE BAG
- A light-weight cotton yarn, each ball approx 1¾oz/164yd (50g/150m):
  - 1 ball in **A**—black
  - 1 ball in **B**—white
- 1 skein (24yd/22m) of No. 5 pearl cotton embroidery thread in red, for 2 tassels
- Sizes D-3 (3.00mm) and E-4 (3.50mm) crochet hooks

### RECTANGULAR BAG
- A light-weight cotton yarn, each ball approx 1¾oz/164yd (50g/150m):
  - 1 ball in **A**—black
  - 1 ball in **B**—white
- 30 wooden beads 7–9mm in diameter
- Sizes D-3 (3.00mm), E-4 (3.50mm), and G-6 (4.00mm) crochet hooks

### BOTH BAGS
- Zipper 8in (20cm) long
- Lining fabric (optional)

## Gauge and finished size
- 22 stitches and 16 rows to 4in (10cm) over pattern st using size D-3 (3.00mm) hook.
- Square bag measures 8in (20cm) square.
- Rectangular bag measures 5in (13cm) tall x 8in (20cm) wide.

## To make square bag
To begin, using size E-4 (3.50mm) hook and A, ch44. (The first row of the pattern must be worked over a multiple of 4ch.)
Change to size D-3 (3.00mm) hook and beg patt as foll:

**Row 1** 1sc in 2nd ch from hook, 1sc in each of rem ch. Turn. (43sc)

**Row 2** Ch1, 1sc in first sc, *1sc in next sc,— ch4, 1sl st in last sc worked (a picot made)—, 1sc in each of next 3sc; rep from * omitting 3sc at end of last rep, insert hook in next sc (which is last sc), yo and draw yarn through, drop A, pick up B and draw yarn through rem 2 loops on hook (color changed). Turn.

**Row 3 (WS)** Ch3, 1sc in first picot, *1dc in each of next 3 free sc, 1sc in next picot; rep from *, ending with 1dc in last sc. Turn.

**Row 4 (RS)** Ch1, 1sc in first dc, *1sc in next sc, 1 picot, 1sc in each of next 3dc; rep from * omitting 3sc at end of last rep, insert hook in 3rd of 3ch, yo and draw yarn through, drop B, pick up A and draw yarn through rem 2 loops on hook (color changed again—always change color in this way). Turn.

**Row 5** As row 3.

**Row 6** As row 4, but dropping A and picking up B.**

Rep rows 3–6 to form patt.

**The rectangular bag (right) has a long beaded strap. Adjust the length of the strap if desired.**

Work in patt until bag measures 16in (40cm) from beg, ending with a 5th patt row (in A).
**Next row** Ch1, 1sc in each st.
Fasten off.

### HANDLE
Using size E-4 (3.50mm) hook and A, ch61—for a 12in (30cm) long handle.
Change to size D-3 (3.00mm) hook and make handle as foll:
**Row 1** 1dc in 4th ch from hook, 1dc in each of rem ch. Turn.
**Row 2** Ch3, skip first dc, 1dc in next dc, 1dc in each of rem dc. Turn.
**Row 3** As row 2.
Fold handle in half lengthwise, bringing foundation-ch edge up level with top of previous row. Then work a row of sc through foundation-ch and top of previous row, but beginning and ending ³⁄₄in (2cm) from end of handle.

### TASSELS
Make two 2³⁄₄in (7cm) long tassels in C as foll:
Wind the thread about 50 times around a piece of cardboard 4in (10cm) wide. Tie one end of the loops together tightly, then cut the other end of the loops to remove the tassel from the cardboard. Bind the tassel together near the top by winding an separate length securely around it. Trim the ends.

### To make rectangular bag
Work as for square bag to **.
Rep rows 3–6 to form patt.
Work in patt until bag measures 10in (26cm) from beg, ending with a 5th patt row (in A).
**Next row** Ch1, 1sc in each st.
Fasten off.

### STRAP
Before beg cord, string 30 beads onto a ball of A so they are ready to use while crocheting strap. Then using size G-6 (4.00mm) hook and 2 strands of A held tog (one strand with beads on and another one without beads), work chain stitches, catching a bead into chain every 2–2¹⁄₂in (5–6cm) by sliding bead up close to work then continuing chain. Work in this way until strap is 48in (122cm) long or desired length (be sure to stretch strap when measuring). Fasten off.

### To finish bags
Fold bag in half, right sides together and overcast stitch side seams. Turn right side out. Secure handle to square bag on outside, overlapping unfolded ends over top of side seams. Secure strap to rectangular bag on inside at side seams.
Backstitch zipper to opening.
Line bag with fabric if desired.
Sew a tassel to square bag below each end of handle.

The square bag on the opposite page has tassels made from a skein of pearl cotton embroidery thread, which gives it a nice sheen to contrast with the more matte finish of the bag yarn.

# Double-crochet scarf

⭐ *This cotton scarf is made with two yarns only, despite its look. One yarn is a plain beige shade, forming intermittant stripes throughout, and the other is a random-dyed yarn in pastel blues and greens. Using a random-dyed yarn is a great way to add lots of color to your crochet with little effort.*

*The simple crochet texture is created by mixing alternating simple single crochet with double crochet.*

## You will need

- 3 x 1³/₄oz/76yd (50g/70m) balls of a random-dyed medium-weight cotton yarn in main color (**MC**)—shades of blues and greens
- 2 x 1³/₄oz/76yd (50g/70m) balls of a medium-weight cotton yarn in contrasting color (**CC**)—beige
- Sizes I-9 (5.50mm) and J-10 (6.00mm) crochet hooks
- 44 beads for fringe

## Gauge and finished size

- 14 stitches to 4in (10cm) over pattern using size I-9 (5.50mm) hook.
- Scarf measures 5³/₄in (14cm) wide x 65in (165cm) long, excluding fringe. Length is adjustable.

## Special note

When working stripe pattern, drop MC at side of work when not in use and pick it up when next needed. But cut off CC after each CC stripe and rejoin when next needed, working over ends to avoid having to weave in later.

## To make scarf

To begin, using size J-10 (6.00mm) hook and CC, make 21ch.

Change to size I-9 (5.50mm) hook and cont.

**Row 1** Using CC, 1sc in 2nd ch from hook, 1sc in each of rem ch, changing to MC with last yo of last sc. Turn. (20sc)

**Row 2** Using MC, ch3 to count as first dc, skip first sc, *1dc in next sc; rep from *. Turn. (20 sts)

**Row 3** Using MC, ch3, skip first dc, *1dc in next dc; rep from *, ending with 1dc in 3rd of 3ch and changing to CC with last yo of last dc. Turn.

**Row 4** Using CC, ch1, 1sc in each dc, ending with 1sc in 3rd of 3ch. Turn. (20sc)

**Row 5** Using CC, ch1, 1sc in each sc, changing to MC with last yo of last sc. Turn.

Rep rows 2–5 to form stripe patt. Work in stripe patt until scarf measures 65in (165cm) or desired length, ending with a row 4. Fasten off.

### BEADED FRINGE

For fringe cut 22 lengths of MC, each 8in (20cm) long. Thread two beads onto each length of MC and knot each end to hold on beads, placing knots about 3¹/₂in (9cm) apart. Trim yarn ends close to knots. Slide one bead up close to each knot.

Attach 11 beaded strands evenly spaced along each end of scarf. To do this, fold a beaded strand in half, then insert hook through edge of scarf and draw the loop at the fold through. Pass the beaded ends through the loop and pull tight to secure.

Choose lightweight beads like these, to make the scarf comfortable and easy to wear. You'll find that bead details are real eyecatchers.

# String bag

✪✪ *This adaptable little shopping bag stretches when filled. It is smartly trimmed with jazzy glass beads. An adaptation of the lacy, circular pattern makes a pretty jug cover or a little mat (see page 51 for instructions and pags 22–23 for tips).*

## You will need

- 1 x 1¾oz/306yd (50g/280m) ball of a No. 10 cotton crochet thread in chosen color
- Size 6 steel (1.50mm) crochet hook
- 12 beads to decorate ends of cords (optional)

## Gauge and finished size

- First 4 rounds of double crochet measure 2in (5cm) in diameter using size 6 steel (1.50mm) hook.
- Bag is approximately 13¾in (35cm) deep, but stretches when filled.

## To make string bag

To begin, ch6 and join with a sl st in first ch to form a ring.

**Round 1 (RS)** Ch3 (these 3ch at beg of dc rounds count as first dc), 11dc in ring, 1sl st in 3rd of first 3ch. Do not turn at end of rounds, but work with RS always facing. (12 sts)

**Round 2** Ch3, 1dc in same place as sl st, 2dc in each of rem dc, 1sl st in 3rd of first 3ch. (24 sts)

**Round 3** As round 2. (48 sts)

**Round 4** Ch3, 1dc in each dc, 1sl st in 3rd of first 3ch.

**Round 5** Ch3, 1dc in same place as sl st, *1dc in next dc, 2dc in next dc; rep from *, ending with 1dc in last dc, 1sl st in 3rd of first 3ch. (72 sts)

**Round 6** Ch3, 1dc in same place as sl st, *1dc in each of next 2dc, 2dc in next dc; rep from *, ending with 1dc in each of last 2dc, 1sl st in 3rd of first 3ch. (96 sts)

**Round 7** As round 4.

**Round 8** Ch3, 1dc in same place as sl st, *1dc in each of next 3dc, 2dc in next dc; rep from *, ending with 1dc in each of last 3dc, 1sl st in 3rd of first 3ch. (120 sts)

**Round 9** Ch1, 1sc in same place as sl st, *ch3, 1sc in next dc, ch5, skip next 2dc, 1sc in next dc; rep from *, ending with ch3, 1sc in next dc, ch2, 1dc in first sc.

**Round 10** Work (1sc, ch3, 1sc) all in loop just formed with ch2 and 1dc, *ch5, (1sc, ch3, 1sc) all in next 5ch-loop; rep from *, ending with ch2, 1dc in first sc. (30 loops, including last loop formed with 2ch and 1dc)

**Round 11** Work (1sc, ch3, 1sc) all in loop just formed, *ch6, (1sc, ch3, 1sc) all in next 5ch-loop; rep from *, ending with ch2, 1tr in first sc.

**Round 12** Work (1sc, ch3, 1sc) all in loop just formed, *ch7, (1sc, ch3, 1sc) all in next 6ch-loop; rep from *, ending with ch3, 1tr in first sc.

**Round 13** Work (1sc, ch3, 1sc) all in loop just formed, *ch8, (1sc, ch3, 1sc) all in next 7ch-loop; rep from *, ending with ch3, 1dtr in first sc.

**Round 14** Work (1sc, ch3, 1sc) all in loop just formed, *ch9, (1sc, ch3, 1sc) all in next 8ch-loop; rep from *, ending with ch4, 1dtr in first sc.

**Round 15** Work (1sc, ch3, 1sc) all in loop just formed, *ch10, (1sc, ch3, 1sc) all in next 9ch-loop; rep from *, ending with ch4, 1trtr in first sc.

**Round 16** Work (1sc, ch3, 1sc) all in loop just formed, *ch11, (1sc, ch3, 1sc) all in next 10ch-loop; rep from *, ending with ch5, 1trtr in first sc.

**Round 17** Work (1sc, ch3, 1sc) all in loop just formed, *ch12, (1sc, ch3, 1sc) all in next 11ch-loop; rep from *, ending with ch5, 1qtr in first sc.

**Round 18** Work (1sc, ch3, 1sc) all in loop just formed, *ch13, (1sc, ch3, 1sc) all in next 12ch-loop; rep from *, ending with ch6, 1qtr in first sc.

**Round 19** Work (1sc, ch3, 1sc) all in loop just formed, *ch13, (1sc, ch3, 1sc) all in next 13ch-loop; rep from *, ending with ch6, 1qtr in first sc.

Rep 19th round 18 times more.

**Next round** 1sc in loop just formed, *ch9, 1sc in next 13ch-loop; rep from *, ending with ch9, 1sl st in first sc.

**Next round** Ch3, *1dc in each of next 9ch, 1dc in next sc; rep from * omitting 1dc at end of last rep, 1sl st in 3rd of first 3ch.

**Next round** Ch1, 1sc in same place as sl st, *ch3, 1sc in each of next 5dc; rep from * omitting 1sc at end of last rep, 1sl st in first sc. Fasten off.

**CORD HANDLES**

Make two cords for the handles of the string bag, each 34in (87cm) long. For an extra-simple cord, make a foundation chain and work one row of single crochet. For the attractive cord shown, using the step-by-step illustrations for guidance, work each of the cords as foll:

To begin, ch2 loosely, then work 1sc in the first ch made (**step 1**), turn, 1sc in foundation loop of 2nd ch made inserting hook in back

of loop (**step 2**), *turn, insert hook in 2 loops at side (**step 3**), yo and draw loop through, yo and draw through 2 loops on hook; rep from * for length required.

Fasten off.

**To finish**

Thread cords alternately through last picot row of bag. Tie ends of each cord together and decorate 4 ends with beads as desired.

**1**

**2**

**3**

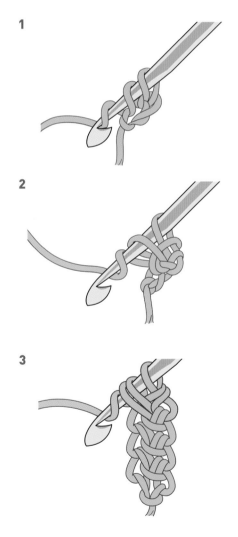

## Traditional jug cover

You can adapt the bag pattern to make a traditional beaded jug cover. It only takes one 1¾oz/306yd (50g/280m) ball of a No. 10 cotton crochet thread and a total of 30 glass beads (twenty 7mm round beads and ten larger beads—the larger ones used here are tubular and measure 9mm in diameter and 10mm long). Make sure the beads you buy have large enough holes for the crochet thread.

### TO MAKE JUG COVER

Before beginning, thread 30 beads onto the crochet thread in reverse order so they are ready to use in the last round. *Thread on two small beads, one large bead; repeat from * until they are all on.

To begin the jug cover, work rounds 1–13 of the pattern for the string bag.

Then work the final round as foll:

**Round 14 (bead round)** Work (1sc, ch3, 1sc) all in loop just formed, *ch7, slide a large bead up close to the hook and ch1 to secure bead, ch7, (1sc, ch3, 1sc) all in next 8ch-loop, [ch4, slide a small bead up close to the hook and ch1 to secure bead, ch4, (1sc, ch3, 1sc) all in next 8ch-loop] twice; rep from *, 1sl st in first sc.

Fasten off.

Weave in any loose ends. Then dampen the cover, pin out, and leave to dry.

# Single-crochet coin purse

✪ *This little purse is made from a basic pattern for working single crochet in the round, so you can adapt it to make other round items—a striped cushion cover for example.*

## You will need

- 2 skeins (each 24yd/22m) of No. 5 pearl cotton embroidery thread in 5 colors:
    - Pale lilac
    - Rose
    - Dusty rose
    - Orange
    - Light purple
- Size 6 steel (1.50mm) crochet hook
- 30 round or square beads, 4–5mm in diameter
- Zipper 6in (15cm) long
- Fabric for lining (optional)

## Gauge and finished size

- Approximately 21 rounds of sc forms a circle 4½in (11.5cm) in diameter using size 6 steel (1.50mm) hook.
- Finished coin purse measures 5in (12.5cm) in diameter.

## Special notes

- To keep track of where the crochet rounds start and finish, position a strand of contrasting yarn at the end of each round. To do this, before starting the next round, place the contrasting strand across the crochet fabric from front to back, close up against the loop on the hook and *above the working yarn*. Next, start to work the first single crochet of the following round, catching the marker in position. The marker marks the start of the round and is caught under the top of the first stitch of the round.
- To change to a new color, drop the color you are working with when there are two loops on the hook and complete the sc with the new color. Work over the ends of the threads to avoid having to weave them in later.

## To make coin purse

The coin purse is made from two circular pieces and the colors are used at random.

**FRONT**

To begin, using size 6 steel (1.50mm) hook and chosen color, ch4 and join with a sl st in first ch to form a ring.

**Round 1 (RS)** Ch1, 8sc in ring. (Do not turn at end of rounds, but work with RS always facing.)

Position marker as explained in Special Note above.

**Round 2** 2sc in each sc. (16sc)

**Round 3** *1sc in next sc, 2sc in next sc; rep from *. (24sc)

Change colors throughout as desired (see Special Note) **and at the same time** work the circle patt as foll:

**Round 4** 1sc in each sc.

**Round 5** *1sc in next sc, 2sc in next sc; rep from *. (36sc)

**Round 6** As round 4.

**Round 7** *1sc in each of next 2sc, 2sc in next sc; rep from *. (48sc)

**Round 8** As round 4.

**Round 9** *1sc in each of next 3sc, 2sc in next sc; rep from *. (60sc)

**Round 10** As round 4.

**Round 11** *1sc in each of next 4sc, 2sc in next sc; rep from *. (72sc)

**Round 12** As round 4.

**Round 13** *1sc in each of next 5sc, 2sc in next sc; rep from *. (84sc)

**Round 14** As round 4.

Cont in this way, adding 12 extra sc in every alternate round and working in random stripes until the coin purse measures 4½in (11.5cm) in diameter (about 21 rounds), ending with an increase round.

Work 1sl st in next st and fasten off.

**BACK**

Make as for front, working random stripes or matching them to front.

**To finish**

Weave in loose ends and press each piece lightly on WS.

**BEAD EDGING**

Thread 30 beads onto the yarn so they are ready to use while crocheting. Holding the two circles with wrong sides together, work the bead edging through both layers as foll:

Insert the hook in a sc through both circles, yo and draw yarn through, ch1, 1sc in same sc as ch was worked, 1sc in next sc, *slide bead up close to hook and ch1, 1sc in each of next 3sc; rep from * until an opening 5½–6in (14–15cm) long (for zipper) remains, then work in sc around opening. Fasten off.

Backstitch zipper to opening.

Line bag with fabric if desired.

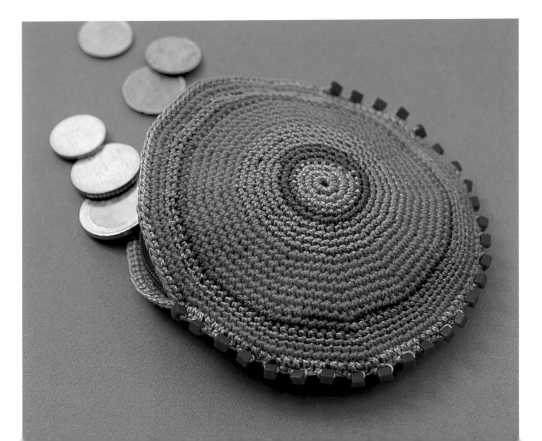

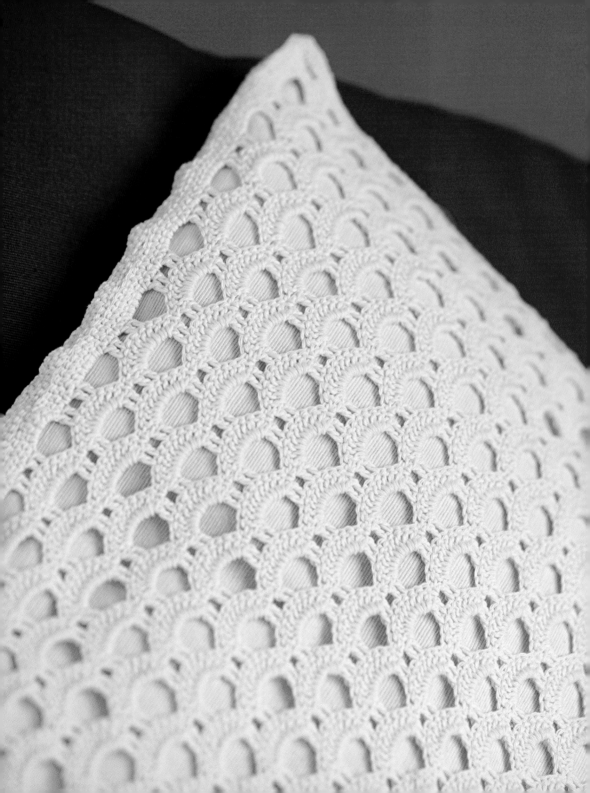

# Scallop cushion

✪ *Quick and easy to make, this cushion cover could be made in any color you like. The lining shows through, so choose a matching one.*

## You will need
• 5 x 1¾oz/164yd (50g/150m) balls of a light-weight cotton yarn in off-white
• Size D-3 (3.00mm) crochet hook
• Covered cushion 18in (45cm) square in desired background color

## Gauge and finished size
• Each scallop repeat measures 1½in (3.5cm) wide and ¾in (2cm) deep.
• Crocheted cover measures 18in (45cm) square, not including edging.

## To make cushion cover
The cushion cover is made from two identical pieces.

### FRONT AND BACK (BOTH ALIKE)
To begin, ch119. (The first row of the pattern is worked over a multiple of 9ch, plus 2ch extra.)

**Row 1** 1sc in 2nd ch from hook, 1sc in each of next 2ch, *ch5, skip next 4ch, 1sc in each of next 5ch; rep from * omitting 5sc at end of last rep, 1sc in each of last 3ch. Turn.

**Row 2 (RS)** Ch1, 1sc in first sc, *9dc in next 5ch-loop, skip next 2sc, 1sc in next sc; rep from *. Turn.

**Row 3** Ch6, skip first sc and first 2dc, *1dc in each of next 2dc, ch1, skip next dc, 1dc in each of next 2dc, ch5, skip next 5 sts; rep from * omitting ch5 at end of last rep, ch2, skip next 2 sts, 1tr in last sc. Turn.

**Row 4** Ch3, 4dc in first 2ch-sp, *1sc in next 1ch-sp, 9dc in next 5ch-loop; rep from * to last 1ch-sp, 1sc in last 1ch-sp, 4dc in last loop, 1dc in 4th of 6ch. Turn.

**Row 5** Ch3, skip first dc, 1dc in each of next 2dc, *ch5, skip next 5 sts, 1dc in each of next 2dc, ch1, skip next dc, 1dc in each of next 2dc; rep from *, ending with ch5, skip next 5 sts, 1dc in each of next 2dc, 1dc in 3rd of 3ch. Turn.

**Row 6** Ch1, 1sc in first dc, *9dc in next 5ch-loop, 1sc in next 1ch-sp; rep from * to last 5ch-loop, 9dc in last 5ch-loop, skip next 2dc, 1sc in 3rd of 3ch. Turn.

Rep rows 3–6 to form patt. Cont in patt until front measures 18in (45cm) from beg, ending with a 3rd or 5th patt row. Fasten off.

### EDGING
Work a sc edging around front as foll:

**Round 1** With RS facing, insert hook through edge of front at any corner, yo and draw yarn through, ch1, 1sc in same place as ch was worked; then working 3sc in each corner, work sc evenly around edge of front and join with a sl st in first sc. (Do not turn at end of rounds, but work with RS always facing.)

**Round 2 (RS)** Ch1, 1sc in same place as sl st, then work 1sc in each sc along sides and 3sc in each corner sc, and join with a sl st in first sc. Fasten off.

## To finish
Weave in any loose ends. With wrong sides facing and stitching just below edging, sew front and back together around three sides. Insert covered cushion and finish seam.

# Single-crochet scarf

✪ *Worked lengthwise in single crochet, this soft, cosy cotton scarf is very easy and quick to make. It is trimmed with a self-fringe of twisted strands.*

## You will need

- A medium-weight cotton yarn, each ball approx 1¾oz/76yd (50g/70m):
    - 3 balls in main color (**MC**)—beige
    - 1 ball each in 4 contrasting colors:
    - **A**—coral; **B**—brick; **C**—purple; **D**—orange
- Sizes I-9 (5.50mm) and J-10 (6.00mm) crochet hooks

## Gauge and finished size

- 13 stitches and 15 rows to 4in (10cm) over sc using size I-9 (5.50mm) hook.
- Scarf measures 6in (15cm) x 66in (165cm).

## To make scarf

The scarf is worked from end to end instead of from side to side in order to create stripes that run lengthwise.

Each row of the scarf is worked with a new strand of yarn, so that there are loose ends of yarn at each end to make a twisted fringe. To begin, using size J-10 (6.00mm) hook and MC and leaving a 10in (25cm) long loose end, ch215. Cut off MC, again leaving a 10in (25cm) loose end, and fasten off by pulling the end through the last ch.

Change to size I-9 (5.50mm) hook and cont.

**Row 1** Using MC again and leaving a 10in (25cm) loose end at edge, insert hook through first ch, yo and draw yarn through, ch1, 1sc in first ch (same ch as hook was first inserted), 1sc in each of rem ch. Turn. (215sc)

Cut off MC, leaving a 10in (25cm) loose end, and fasten off by pulling the end through the last sc.

**Row 2** Using A and leaving a long loose end at edge as before, insert hook through first sc, yo and draw yarn through, ch1, 1sc in first sc (same sc as ch was worked), 1sc in each of rem sc. Turn.

Cut off A, leaving a 10in (25cm) loose end, and fasten off as before.

Rep 2nd row 21 times more **and at the same time** leaving long loose ends at each end of every row as before, work 21-row stripe sequence as foll:

1 row B, 1 row C, 1 row B, 1 row A, 3 rows MC, 1 row D, 5 rows MC, 1 row A, 1 row B, 1 row A, 2 rows MC, 1 row D, 2 rows MC.

Fasten off.

### TWISTED FRINGE

Each strand of twisted fringe is made up of two loose ends of yarn. To make the twisted fringe, first knot the strands together two at a time across each end, close to the edge of the crochet. Then take one pair of knotted strands and twist each strand individually in the same direction until it starts to kink.

Place the twisted strands together and twist them both in the opposite direction so they wrap around each other. Knot the end of the twisted pair 3in (7.5cm) from the edge of the crochet and trim the end. Do the same with each pair of strands.

# Cotton afghan

✪✪ *These cotton crochet afghan squares are worked in four simple rounds. Use them for a throw, as per instructions, or a cushion cover.*

## You will need
- A medium-weight cotton yarn, each ball approx 1³⁄₄oz/76yd (50g/70m):
    9 balls for center color of motif (**A**)— light blue
    14 balls for middle color of motif (**B**)— purple
    20 balls for border color of motif (**C**)— mid blue
- Size G-6 (4.00mm) crochet hook

## Gauge and finished size
- Each motif measures 5in (12.5cm) square.
- Afghan measures 50in (125cm) x 70in (175cm).

## Special note
Work over the loose ends of the yarn to avoid lots of weaving in ends later.

## To make afghan
The afghan is made up of 140 motifs. (You can make more motifs to alter the size, but this will alter the amount of yarn required.)

### MOTIF
To begin, using A ch8 and join with a sl st in first ch to form a ring.

**Round 1 (RS)** Ch3, 1dc in ring, (ch7, 1sl st in top of last dc, 5dc in ring) 3 times, ch7, 1sl st in top of last dc, 3dc in ring, 1sl st in 3rd of first 3ch. Fasten off.

**Round 2** With RS facing and using B, insert hook through first 7ch-loop made on previous round, yo and draw yarn through (place this 'joining' st at base of 7ch-loop on right-hand side), ch4, work [2dc, (ch3, 3dc) 3 times] all in same 7ch-loop, *skip next free dc on first round, 1sl st in each of next 2dc, work [(3dc, ch3) 3 times, 3dc] all in next 7ch-loop; rep from *, ending with skip 1dc, 1sl st in each of next 2dc, 1sl st in 4th of first 4ch. Fasten off.

**Round 3** With RS facing and using C, insert hook through first 3ch-loop made on previous round, yo and draw yarn through, ch1, 1sc in same loop, *ch4, work (1sc, ch3, 1sc) all in next 3ch-loop, ch4, 1sc in next 3ch-loop, ch5, 1sc in next 3ch-loop; rep from * omitting 1sc at end of last rep, 1sl st in first sc. Do not turn.

**Round 4** Ch3, *4dc in next 4ch-loop, 1dc in next sc, work (2dc, ch2, 2dc) all in next 3ch-loop, 1dc in next sc, 4dc in next 4ch-loop, 1dc in next sc, ch1, 1sc in next 5ch-sp, ch1, 1dc in next sc; rep from * omitting 1dc at end of last rep, 1sl st in 3rd of first 3ch. Fasten off. Make 139 more motifs.

## To finish
Weave in any loose ends.Using C, overcast stitch squares together, first joining 14 rows of 10 motifs each, then joining the rows.

### EDGING
With RS facing and using B, work sc evenly around edge, working 1sc in each stitch and each chain space, and working 3sc in each corner. At end of round, join with a sl st to first sc. Fasten off.

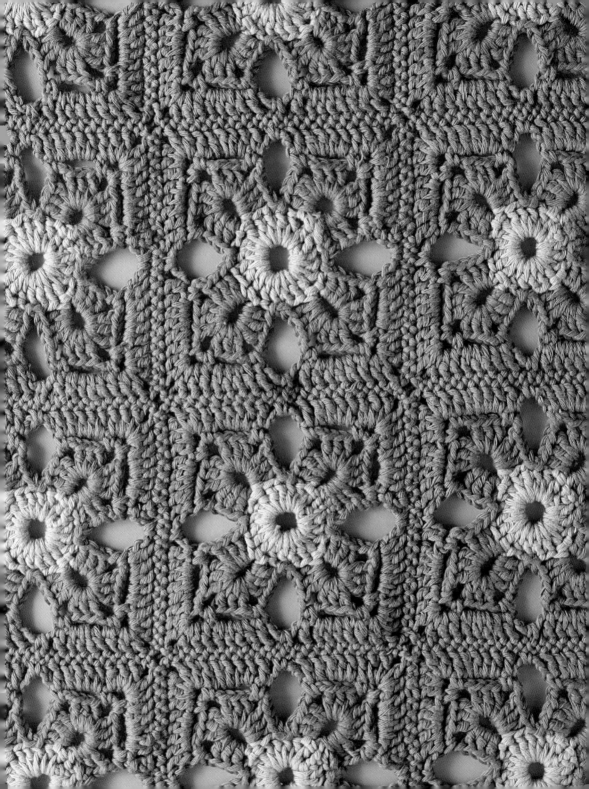

# Wool afghan

✪✪ *The instructions here are for an afghan but you could make just a few squares and make a cushion cover instead. The color scheme here is created from a 9-square repeat.*

## You will need
- A wool-mix, medium-weight yarn, each ball approx 1¾oz/131yd (50g/120m):
    10 balls in main color used for border row of each motif (**MC**)—black
    5 balls in first contrasting color (**A**)—light rose
    5 balls in second contrasting color (**B**)—mid rose
    5 balls in third contrasting color (**C**)—gray
- Size H-8 (5.00mm) crochet hook

## Gauge and finished size
- Each motif measures 3¾in (9.5cm) square.
- Afghan measures 45in (114cm) x 60in (152cm).

## To make afghan
The afghan is made up of 192 motifs. (You can make more or fewer motifs to alter the size, but this will alter the amount of yarn required.)

### MOTIF
To begin, using A ch6 and join with a sl st in first ch to form a ring.
**Round 1 (RS)** Using A, ch3, 1dc in ring, (ch1, 2dc in ring) 3 times, ch1, 1sl st in 3rd of first 3ch. Fasten off.
Working with RS always facing, cont as foll:
**Round 2** Using B, insert hook through first

1ch-sp made on previous round, yo and draw yarn through—called *join with a sl st—*, ch3, work (1dc, ch1, 2dc) all in same 1ch-sp, *(ch1, 2dc) twice in each of next 3 1ch-sps, ch1, 1sl st in 3rd of first 3ch. Fasten off.
**Round 3** Using C, join with a sl st in first 1ch-sp made on previous round, ch3, work (1dc, ch1, 2dc) all in same 1ch-sp, *(ch1, 2dc) twice in each of next 7 1ch-sps, ch1, 1sl st in 3rd of first 3ch. Fasten off.
**Round 4** Using MC, join with a sl st in first 1ch-sp made on previous round, ch3, 2dc in same 1ch-sp (corner), *(ch1, 2dc) in each of next 3 1ch-sps, ch1, 3dc in next 1ch-sp (corner); rep from * 3 times, omitting 3dc at end of last rep, 1sl st in 3rd of first 3ch. Fasten off.
Make 191 more motifs, using a different color for each round and always using MC for round 4, but using random colors (A, B, or C) for rounds 1–3.

## To finish
Weave in any loose ends.
Pin out each motif with WS face up and press following instructions on yarn label.
Arrange motifs and using MC, overcast stitch squares together, first joining 12 rows of 16 motifs each, then joining the rows.

### EDGING
With RS facing and using MC, work sc evenly around edge, working 1sc in each dc and each ch-sp, and working 3sc in each of four corners of afghan. At end of round, join with a sl st in first sc. Fasten off.

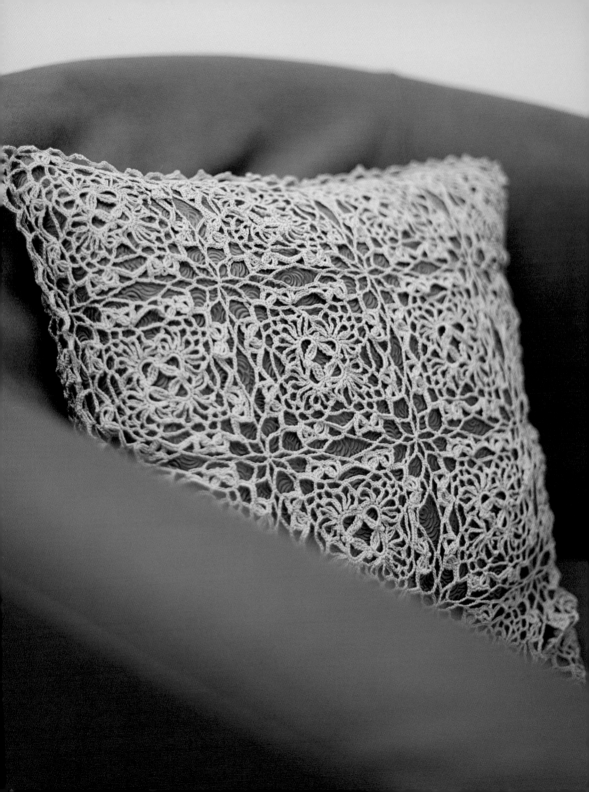

# Lacy cushion

✪✪✪ *This cushion cover is a test of your crocheting skills! It has a crocheted back and front, joined together with a pretty edging to give a decorative finish. The cover is made up of lace squares which are crocheted together.*

## You will need

- 6 x ³/₄oz/158yd (20g/145m) balls of a No. 20 cotton crochet thread in chosen color (6 motifs can be worked from one ball)
- Size 7 steel (1.25mm) crochet hook
- Covered cushion 15³/₄in (40cm) square in desired background color

## Gauge and finished size

- Each motif measures 4in (10cm) square.
- Crocheted cover measures 40cm (15³/₄in) square, excluding edging.

## To make cushion cover

The cushion cover is made from two identical square pieces.

### FRONT AND BACK (BOTH ALIKE)

Front and back are each made up of 16 motifs.

### FIRST MOTIF

To begin, ch10.

**Round 1 (RS)** *Leaving last loop of each dtr on hook work 3dtr in 10th ch from hook, yo and draw through all 4 loops on hook (a 3dtr cluster made), ch11; rep from * 3 times more working ch1 instead of ch11 at end of last rep, 1sl st in same ch as base of first cluster. (Do not turn at end of rounds, but work with RS always facing.)

**Round 2** *12sc in next loop (this chain loop is along edge of dtr cluster), 1sc in next 1ch-sp (between cluster groups), ch4, 1sl st in last sc (a picot made); rep from *, ending with 1sl st in first sc. (4 12sc scallops)

**Round 3** 1sl st in each of next 3sc, ch1, 1sc in same place as last sl st, *(ch13, 1sc in next sc) 5 times, ch7, skip first 3sc of next scallop, 1sc in next sc; rep from * omitting 1sc at end of last rep, 1sl st in first sc.

**Round 4** 1sl st in each of first 5ch of first 13ch-loop, 3sc in same loop, *(ch5, 3sc in next 13ch-loop) 4 times, 1tr in next 7ch-loop, 3sc in next 13ch-loop; rep from * omitting 3sc at end of last rep, 1sl st in first sc.

**Round 5** 1sl st in each of next 2sc and 2ch, 1sc in loop, *ch5, work [(1dc, ch5, 1dc) in next 5ch-loop] twice, ch5, 1sc in next 5ch-loop, ch9, 1sc in next 5ch-loop; rep from * omitting 1sc at end of last rep, 1sl st in first sc.

**Round 6** 1sl st in each of next 2ch, 1sc in loop, *(ch6, a 3tr cluster in 6th ch from hook) twice (a cluster loop made), 1sc in next 5ch-loop, ch9, 1sc in next 5ch-loop, 1 cluster loop, 1sc in next 5ch-loop, ch11, skip next 9ch-loop, 1sc in next 5ch-loop; rep from * omitting 1sc at end of last rep, 1sl st in first sc.

**Round 7** *Work (4sc, ch3, 4sc) in next loop (this chain loop is at edge of cluster), ch3, (4sc, ch3, 4sc) in next loop, (5sc, ch5, 5sc) in next 9ch-loop (this forms corner scallop), (4sc, ch3, 4sc) in next loop, ch3, (4sc, ch3, 4sc) in next loop, 13sc in next 11ch-loop; rep from *, ending with 1sl st in first sc.

**Round 8** 1sl st in each of next 3sc and 1ch, 1sc in 3ch-loop, *ch9, skip next 3ch-loop

(loop between scallops), 1sc in next 3ch-loop, ch7, (1tr, ch7, 1tr) in next 5ch-loop (**corner loop made**), ch7, 1sc in next 3ch-loop, ch9, skip next 3ch-loop, 1sc in next 3ch-loop, ch4, skip next 10sc, 1sc in next sc (center sc of 13-sc group), ch4, 1sc in next 3ch-loop; rep from * omitting 1sc at end of last rep, 1sl st in first sc. Fasten off.

### SECOND MOTIF

Work as first motif for 7 rounds, then join to first motif on round 8. When joining motifs, hold them with wrong sides together, stitches aligned, and second motif in front. Begin the round working on the second motif only and join to first when indicated as foll:
**Round 8 (joining round)** 1sl st in each of next 3sc and 1ch, 1sc in 3ch-loop, ch9, skip next 3ch-loop (loop between scallops), 1sc in next 3ch-loop, ch7, 1tr in next 5ch-loop, ch3, 1sc in a corresponding 7ch-corner-loop on first motif, ch3, 1tr in same 5ch-loop on second motif, ch3, 1sc in next 7ch-loop on first motif, ch3, 1sc in next 3ch-loop on second motif, ch4, 1sc in next 9ch-loop on first motif, ch4, skip next 3ch-loop on second motif, 1sc in next 3ch-loop on second motif, ch4, skip next 10sc on second motif and work 1sc in next sc, ch4, 1sc in next 3ch-loop on second motif, ch4, 1sc in next 9ch-loop on first motif, ch4, skip next 3ch-loop on second motif and work 1sc in next 3ch-loop, ch3, 1sc in next 7ch-loop on first motif, ch3, 1tr in next 5ch-loop on second motif, ch3, 1sc in next 7ch-corner-loop on first motif, ch3, 1tr in same 5ch-loop on second motif and complete as round 8 of first motif (from where it says "corner loop made").
Make 4 rows of 4 motifs, joining each as second motif was joined to first. Where 4 corners meet, join third and fourth motifs to joining of previous motifs.
Dampen, pin out, and leave to dry.

### To finish

Place back and front with wrong sides together and join together while working edging as foll:
### EDGING
**Round 1** Working through both sections, attach crochet thread to second loop to right of any free corner loop, 1sc in same place as join, ch9, 1sc in next loop, ch19, **work (1sc, ch5, 1sc) in next corner loop, *(ch9, 1sc in next loop) twice, ch9,—leaving the last loop of each dc on hook and working in front section only, skip next sc, 1dc in next sc on front section and 1dc in corresponding sc on back section, yo and draw through all 3 loops on hook (a joint dc made)—, (ch9, working through both sections work 1sc in next loop) twice, ch9, 1sc in next join of motifs; rep from * 3 times more omitting 1sc at end of last rep; rep from ** twice more, work (1sc, ch5, 1sc) in next corner loop, (ch9, 1sc in next loop) twice, ***ch9, working in front section only, skip next sc, 1dc in next sc, (ch9, 1sc in next loop) twice, ch9, 1sc in next join of motifs (ch9, 1sc in next loop) twice; rep from *** twice more, ch9, skip next sc, 1dc in next sc, ch9, 1sl st in first sc.
**Round 2** Work (5sc, ch3, 5sc) in each of next 2 loops, *work (3sc, ch3, 3sc) in next 5ch-loop, work (5sc, ch3, 5sc) in each 9ch-loop along side; rep from * 3 times more, ending with 1sl st in first sc. Fasten off.
Dampen and press edging.
Insert covered cushion and sew together opening.

Each motif of the Lacy Cushion is joined to its neighbor in the 8th round. This close-up shows the crochet stitches that join four motifs where they meet at a corner to create a star shape.

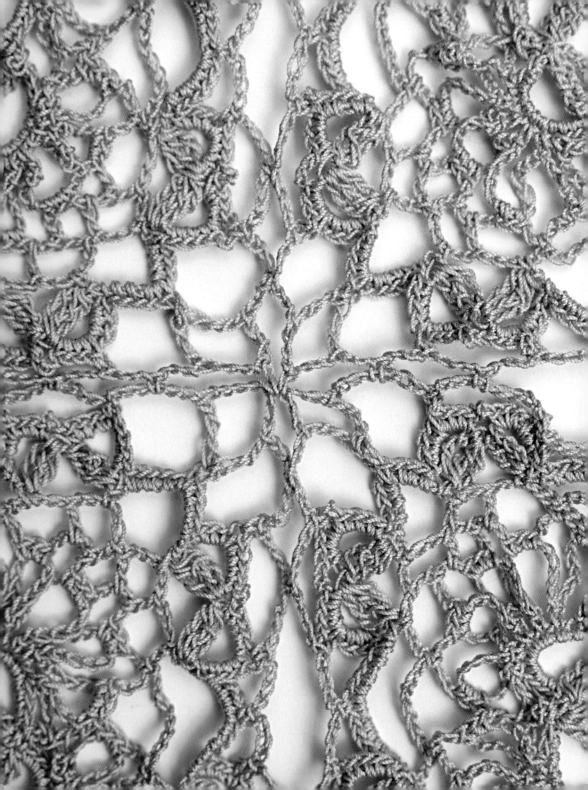

# Hand towel edging

✪✪ *This simple edging adorns a cotton piqué guest towel, but you could, just as easily, use it for a pillowcase, if you prefer. The edging is made separately then stitched in place, and you can adjust the length to suit that of your own towel. Fine white cotton crochet thread has been used to make the scallops, although a heavier weight yarn or a colored one would work equally well.*

## You will need
- 1 x 1³/₄oz/219yd (50g/200m) ball of a No. 5 cotton crochet thread in chosen color
- Size 6 steel (1.50mm) crochet hook
- Hand towel of your choice

## Gauge and finished size
- The edging measures 1¹/₂in (4cm) deep (once blocked) and each pattern repeat measures 1¹/₂in (4cm) across. Finished length is adjustable.

## To make edging
Before beginning, calculate how many scallops are needed to fit your towel.
To begin, ch14 for each pattern repeat needed except the last, and make 13ch more for the last pattern repeat. (The first row is worked over a multiple of 14ch, plus 13ch extra.) The edging shown is 12in (32cm) long and the foundation chain needed for this length is 111ch.
**Row 1 (RS)** 1sc in 2nd ch from hook, 1sc in each of rem ch. Turn. (110sc)
**Row 2** Ch1, 1sc in each of first 4sc, ch5, skip next 4sc, 1sc in next sc, *(ch3, skip next 2sc,

1sc in next sc) 3 times, ch5, skip next 4sc, 1sc in next sc; rep from * to last 3sc, 1sc in each of last 3sc. Turn.
**Row 3** Ch1, 1sc in first sc, *(5dc, ch5, 5dc) all in first 5ch-loop (a scallop made), (1sc in next 3ch-loop, ch3) twice, 1sc in next 3ch-loop; rep from * to last 5ch-loop, 1 scallop in last 5ch-loop, skip next 3sc, 1sc in last sc. Turn.
**Row 4** Ch5, (1sc, ch3, 1sc) all in 5ch-loop of first scallop, *ch2, 1tr in next 3ch-loop, ch11, 1tr in next 3ch-loop, ch2, (1sc, ch3, 1sc) all in 5ch-loop of next scallop; rep from *, ending with 1dtr in last sc. Turn.
**Row 5** Ch1, (1sc, ch3, 1sc) all in first 3ch-loop, *15dc in next 11ch-loop, (1sc, ch3, 1sc) all in next 3ch-loop; rep from * to end.
Fasten off.
Dampen edging, pin out, and leave to dry.
Sew edging to one end of hand towel.

Made in only five rows, this edging is quite easy to make. If you're looking for an alternative edging, turn to pages 26 and 27 and take your pick. You'll find some even simpler edgings there.

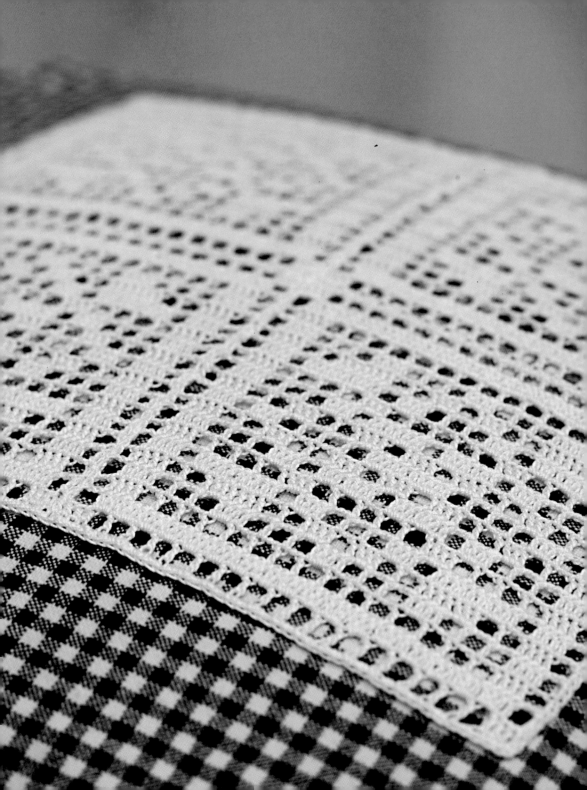

# Filet pillow

✪✪ *Four blocks of filet crochet form the centerpiece of a gingham cushion, but you could also create an entire cushion from similar squares, which are joined together. Then add the filet edging shown on page 71 as a border if you wish.*

## You will need
- 1 x ¾oz/158yd (20g/145m) ball of a No. 20 cotton crochet thread in chosen color
- Size 7 steel (1.25mm) crochet hook
- Covered cushion of desired size

## Gauge and finished size
- 20 sps and 20 rows to 4in (10cm) using size 7 steel (1.25mm) hook.
- Each motif measures 3¾in (9.5cm) square.
- Four joined motifs measure 7½in (19cm) square.

## Special note
Filet crochet is made up of spaces (sps) and blocks (blks) of double crochet stitches. Start the pattern following the written instructions to see how the blocks and spaces are made and then continue working from the chart alone (turn to page 25 for the chart).

## To make filet for pillow
The filet for the pillow is made from 4 motifs.
### MOTIF
To begin, ch60.
**Row 1** 1dc in 4th ch from hook, 1dc in each of next 2ch, (ch2, skip next 2ch, 1dc in next ch) 17 times (17 sps made), 1dc in each of next 3ch. Turn.

**Row 2** Ch5, skip first 3dc, 1dc in next dc (sp made at beg of row), (2dc in next 2ch-sp, 1dc in next dc) 17 times (17 blks made over 17 sps), ch2, skip next 2dc, 1dc in next ch (sp made over blk at end of row). Turn.

**Row 3** Ch5, skip first dc, 1dc in next dc (sp made over sp at beg of row), 1dc in each of next 3dc (1 blk made over 1 blk), (ch2, skip next 2dc, 1dc in next dc) 15 times (15 sps made over 15 blks), 1 blk, ch2, skip next 2ch, 1dc in next ch (sp made over sp at end of row). Turn.

Continue to follow diagram from 4th to 18th row (see page 25).

**19th row** Ch3, 2dc in first sp, 1dc in next dc (blk made at beg of row), 17 sps, 2dc in next sp, 1dc in 3rd of 5ch (blk made at end of row). Fasten off.

Make 3 motifs more in same way.

## To finish
Weave in loose ends.
Overcast stitch four motifs neatly together, making two rows of two motifs.
### EDGING
Work a row of sc evenly around edge, working 3sc in each corner and ending with a sl st in first sc. Fasten off.
Dampen crochet, pin out, and leave to dry.
Stitch to center of cushion cover.

# Pillowcase edgings

✪✪ *These little lace edgings are ideal for a pillowcase. One has simple picots, the other is an uncomplicated filet design. Adjust the length and colors to suit your own bed linens, and if you wish, use a finer thread (such as gauge 20), with a finer hook (size 7 steel/1.25mm).*

## You will need
- 1 x 1³/₄oz/306yd (50g/280m) ball of a No. 10 cotton crochet thread in chosen color
- Size 6 steel (1.50mm) crochet hook
- Pillowcase of your choice

## Gauge and finished size
- **FILET EDGING**
  The filet edging measures 1¹/₂in (3.5cm) deep, and there are 15 rows to 4in (10cm) using size 6 steel (1.50mm) hook.
  Can be worked to required length.
- **PICOT EDGING**
  The picot edging measures 1¹/₂in (3.5cm) deep and each scallop repeat measures 1in (2.5cm) across using size 6 steel (1.50mm) hook.
  Length is adjustable.

## To make filet edging
To begin, ch20.
**Row 1** 1dc in 8th ch from hook, *ch2, skip next 2ch, 1dc in next ch; rep from *. Turn.
**Row 2** Ch5, skip first dc, 1dc in next dc, (2dc in next 2ch-sp, 1dc in next dc) 3 times, ch2, skip next 2ch, 1dc in next ch. Turn.
**Row 3** Ch5, skip first dc, 1dc in each of next 4dc, ch2, skip next 2ch, 1dc in each of next 4dc, ch2, skip next 2ch, 1dc in next ch. Turn.
**Row 4** Ch5, skip first dc, 1dc in each of next 4dc, 2dc in next 2ch-sp, 1dc in each of next 4dc, ch2, skip next 2ch, 1dc in next ch. Turn.
**Row 5** Ch5, skip first dc, 1dc in next dc, (ch2, skip next 2dc, 1dc in next dc) 3 times, ch2, skip next 2ch, 1dc in next ch. Turn.
Rep rows 2–5 until edging is required length, ending with a 4th patt row.
Fasten off.

## To make picot edging
Before beginning, calculate how many picoted scallops are needed to fit your pillowcase.
Make 10ch for each scallop needed, then make 3ch extra for edge stitches. (The first row is worked over a multiple of 10ch, plus 3ch extra.) The edging shown is 16in (40cm) long and the foundation chain needed for this length is 163ch.
**Row 1 (RS)** 1sc in 2nd ch from hook, 1sc in each of rem ch. Turn.
**Row 2** Ch1, 1sc in each of first 2sc, ch2, skip next 2sc, 1sc in next sc, *ch9, skip next 2sc, 1sc in next sc, ch2, skip next 2sc, 1sc in each of next 2sc, ch2, skip next 2sc, 1sc in next sc; rep from * to last 7sc, ch9, skip next 2sc, 1sc in next sc, ch2, skip next 2sc, 1sc in each of last 2sc. Turn.
**Row 3** Ch1, 1sc in each of first 2sc, work [(3dc, ch3) 3 times, 3dc] all in next 9ch-loop, skip next sc, *1sc in each of next 2sc, work [(3dc, ch3) 3 times, 3dc] all in next 9ch-loop, skip next sc; rep from *, ending with 1sc in each of last 2sc. Turn.

**Row 4** Ch4, 1sc in first 3ch-loop, ch4, work (1sc, ch3, 1sc) all in next 3ch-loop, *ch4, 1sc in each of next 2 3ch-loops, ch4, work (1sc, ch3, 1sc) all in next 3ch-loop; rep from *, ending with ch4, 1sc in next 3ch-loop, ch4, 1sl st in last sc. Turn.
**5th row** *(5sc in next 4ch-loop) twice, work [(1sc, ch3) 3 times, 1sc] all in next 3ch-loop; rep from *, ending with work (5sc in next 4ch-loop) twice.
Fasten off.

## To finish edgings

Dampen edging, pin out, and leave to dry. Sew edge of crochet edging to edge of pillowcase with matching thread.

# Christmas decorations

✪✪✪ *These little motifs make great Christmas decorations (suitably stiffened and hung on pretty ribbons), but you could alternatively hang them on cupboard doors or at the window. Adding beads or using metallicized yarns gives them a festive touch. Once made, they will need to be stiffened with a sugar solution or with starch.*

## You will need

- 1 x ¾oz/158yd (20g/145m) ball of a No. 20 cotton crochet thread in white (one ball will make all four decorations)
- Size 7 steel (1.25mm) crochet hook
- Beads to decorate—8 for eight-pointed star, 6 for six-pointed star, 4 for diamond
- Narrow ribbon for hanging

## Finished sizes

- Six-pointed star measures 3½in (9cm) in diameter.
- Eight-pointed star measures 3in (7.5cm) in diameter.
- Diamond measures 3in (7.5cm) square.
- Snowflake measures 3¾in (9.5cm) in diameter.

## To make eight-pointed star

Before beginning, thread 8 beads onto the crochet thread.
To begin, ch16 and join with a sl st in first ch to form a ring.
**Round 1 (RS)** 32sc in ring, 1sl st in first sc. (Do not turn as end of rounds, but work with RS always facing.)
**Round 2** Ch1, 1sc in same place as sl st, *ch15, 1sc in each of next 2sc; rep from * omitting 1sc at end of last rep, 1sl st in first sc. (16 15ch-loops)
**Round 3** 1sl st in each of first 6ch of first 15ch-loop, ch1, 3sc in same loop, *ch2, work (1sc, ch5, 1tr, ch5, 1sc) all in next loop, ch2, 3sc in next loop; rep from * omitting 3sc at end of last rep, 1sl st in first sc of first 3sc group.
**Round 4** 1sl st in next sc, ch6, *1sc in next 2ch-sp, work (1sc, 1hdc, 5dc) all in next 5ch-loop, 1dc in next tr, work (5dc, 1hdc, 1sc) all in next 5ch-loop, 1sc in next 2ch-sp, ch3, skip next sc, 1dc in next sc (center sc of 3sc group), ch3; rep from * omitting 1dc and ch3 at end of last rep, 1sl st in 3rd of first 6ch.
**Round 5 (bead round)** Ch1, 1sc in same place as sl st, *ch7, work (1sc, ch1, slide bead up close to work, ch2—first of these ch secures bead in place—, 1sc) all in dc at center of next point, ch7, 1sc in dc between next 2 3ch-sps; rep from * omitting 1sc at end of last rep, 1sl st in first sc.
Fasten off.

## To make six-pointed star

Before beginning, thread 6 beads onto the crochet thread.
To begin, ch14 and join with a sl st in first ch to form a ring.
**Round 1 (RS)** 24sc in ring, 1sl st in first sc. (Do not turn as end of rounds, but work with RS always facing.)

Shown from left to right are the eight-pointed star, the six-pointed star, and the diamond motif.

**Round 2** Ch4, 1tr in same place as sl st, *ch3, (2tr in next sc) twice; rep from *, ending with ch3, 2tr in next sc, 1sl st in 4th of first 4ch. (12 3ch-sps)

**Round 3** 1sl st in next tr, 1sl st in first ch of next 3ch-sp, 1sc in same 3ch-sp, *ch4, 1sc in next 3ch-sp; rep from *, ending with ch4, 1sl st in first sc.

**Round 4** *Work (1sc, 1hdc, 3dc, 1hdc, 1sc) all in next 4ch-loop; rep from *, ending with 1sl st in first sc. (12 scallops)

**Round 5** 1sl st in each of next 2 sts, 1sc in next st (center dc of scallop), *ch5,—leaving the last loop of each tr on hook, work 1tr in next dc, skip next 4 sts, 1tr in next st, yo and draw through all 3 loops on hook (a joint tr made)—, ch5, 1sc in next st (center dc of scallop), ch8, skip next 6 sts, 1sc in next st (center dc of scallop); rep from * omitting 1sc at end of last rep, 1sl st in first sc.

**Round 6** 1sl st in first ch of next 5ch-loop, ch3, 7dc in same 5ch-loop, *ch3, 8dc in next 5ch-loop, work (1sc, ch3, 1sc) all in next 8ch-loop, 8dc in next 5ch-loop; rep from * omitting 8dc at end of last rep; 1sl st in 3rd of first 3ch.

**Round 7 (bead round)** 1sl st in each of next 7dc, 1sl st in first ch of next 3ch-loop, ch8, slide bead up close to hook, ch2—first of these ch secures bead in place—, 1sl st in 4th ch from hook, ch2, 1tr in same 3ch-loop, *ch7, work (1sc, ch3, 1sc) all in next 3ch-loop, ch7, work (1tr, ch4, slide bead up close to hook, ch2, 1sl st in 4th ch from hook, ch2, 1tr) all in same 3ch-loop (V-st made); rep from * omitting V-st at end of last rep, 1sl st in 4th of first ch made. Fasten off.

For a glittery effect, make the six-pointed star (foreground) and eight-pointed star (background) in metallic thread and add silver beads.

## To make diamond

Before beginning, thread 4 beads onto the crochet thread.

To begin, ch2.

**Round 1 (RS)** 6sc in 2nd ch from hook, 1sl st in first sc. (Do not turn as end of rounds, but work with RS always facing.)

**Round 2** Ch3 (to count as first dc), 1dc in same place as sl st, 2dc in each of rem 5sc, 1sl st in 3rd of first 3ch. (12 sts)

**Round 3** Ch1, 1sc in same place as sl st, *(ch11, 1sc in next dc) twice, ch17, 1sc in next dc; rep from * omitting 1sc at end of last rep, 1sl st in first sc. (4 17ch-corner-loops and 8 11ch-loops)

**Round 4** 1sl st in each of first 4ch of first 11ch-loop, ch1, 2sc in same loop, *ch2, 2sc in next 11ch-loop, ch6, 3sc in next 17ch-loop, ch6, 2sc in next 11ch-loop; rep from * omitting 2sc at end of last rep, 1sl st in first sc.

**Round 5** 1sl st in next sc, 1sl st in first ch of first 2ch-sp, 1sc in same sp, *ch3, work (1sc, 1hdc, 7dc, 1hdc, 1sc) all in next 6ch-loop, ch3, skip next sc, 1sc in next sc (center sc of 3sc group), ch3, work (1sc, 1hdc, 7dc, 1hdc, 1sc) all in next 6ch-loop, ch3, 1sc in next 2ch-sp; rep from * omitting 1sc at end of last rep, 1sl st in first sc.

**Round 6** 1sl st in first ch of first 3ch-loop, 1sc in same loop, *ch7, work (1tr, ch8, 1sc) all in next 3ch-loop, work (1sc, ch8, 1tr) all in next 3ch-loop, ch7, 1sc in next 3ch-loop, ch3, 1sc in next 3ch-loop; rep from * omitting 1sc at end of last rep, 1sl st in first sc.

**Round 7** *Work [(1sc, 1hdc, 7dc, 1hdc, 1sc) all in next loop] 4 times, work (1sc, ch7, 1sc) all in next loop; rep from *, ending with 1sl st in first sc.

**Round 8** 1sl st in each of next 5 sts, ch1, 1sc in same place as last sl st, *ch7, 1sc in center dc of next scallop, ch7, slide bead up close to hook, ch2—first of these ch secures

bead in place—, 1sl st in 4th ch from hook, ch6, 1sc in center dc of next scallop, ch7, 1sc in center dc of next scallop, ch3, 1sc in next 7ch-loop, ch3, 1sc in center dc of next scallop; rep from * omitting last sc at end of last rep, 1sl st in first sc.
Fasten off.

## To make snowflake

To begin, ch20 and join with a sl st in first ch to form a ring.

**Round 1 (RS)** Ch4 (to count as first tr), 39tr in ring, 1sl st in 4th of first 4ch. (Do not turn as end of rounds, but work with RS always facing.)

**Round 2** Ch1, 1sc in same place as sl st, 1sc in each of next 3tr, *work [(1sc, ch5) 3 times, 1sc] all in front loop only of next tr (a triple picot made), 1sc in each of next 4tr; rep from * omitting 4sc at end of last rep, 1sl st in first sc. (8 triple picots)

**Round 3** Ch1, 1sc in same place as sl st, *ch4, 1tr in each of next 2sc, ch4, 1sc in next sc, working behind next triple picot work 1 triple picot in back loop of next tr on first round, 1sc in first sc of next 4-sc group; rep from * omitting 1sc at end of last rep, 1sl st in first sc.

**Round 4** 1sl st in each of next 4ch and in next tr, ch4, 2tr in same place as last sl st, *ch3, 3tr in next tr, ch5, 3tr in next tr; rep from * omitting 3tr at end of last rep, 1sl st in 4th of first 4ch.

**Round 5** Ch1, 1sc in same place as sl st, 1sc in each of next 2tr, *3sc in next 3ch-sp, 1sc in each of next 3tr, 5sc in next 5ch-sp, 1sc in each of next 3tr; rep from * omitting 3sc at end of last rep, 1sl st in first sc.

**Round 6** Ch1, 1sc in same place as sl st, 1sc in each of next 3sc, *work 1 triple picot in front loop only of next sc, 1sc in each of next 4sc, ch7, skip next 5sc, 1sc in each of next

4sc; rep from * omitting 4sc at end of last rep, 1sl st in first sc.

**Round 7** Ch1, 1sc in same place as sl st, 1sc in each of next 3sc, *work 1 triple picot in back loop of next sc on round 5, 1sc in each of next 4sc, ch5, 1sc in next 7ch-loop, ch5, 1sc in each of next 4sc; rep from * omitting 4sc at end of last rep, 1sl st in first sc.

**Round 8** Ch1, 1sc in same place as sl st, *ch9, 1sl st in 4th ch from hook, ch6, skip (3sc, a triple picot, and 3sc) and work 1sc in next sc, ch7,—leaving the last loop of each tr on hook work 1tr in each of next 2 5ch-loops, yo and draw through all 3 loops on hook (a joint tr made)—, ch7, 1sc in next sc; rep from * omitting 1sc at end of last rep, 1sl st in first sc.
Fasten off.

## To finish all decorations

Weave in loose ends.

To stiffen the crochet decorations, starch them. Alternatively, mix 3 tablespoons sugar with 1/2 cup water, bring to a boil while stirring, then leave to cool. Dip the crochet in this sugar-water bath and shake out excess water. Pin out carefully and leave to dry.

Use lengths of ribbon to hang the decorations. Loop the center of the ribbon through the edge of the decoration and tie the ends together.

For an interesting alternative hanging cord, crochet a beaded one. Simply thread small beads onto the crochet cotton, then work a length of chain, sliding a bead into place on every 4th or 5th chain.

**The snowflake motif is adorned with delicate little three-dimensional flowers that are made as the rounds are worked, of loops of chain stitches.**

# Suppliers

For stockists and suppliers of yarns, contact your local craft,
needlework, or fabric store or contact the companies below.
If you want to find stockists in other countries, contact the main
Coats Crafts UK website, below.

Coats and Clark
Consumer services
PO Box 12229
Greenville, South Carolina 29612-0229
(800)648 1479
www.coatsandclark.com

Coats Crafts UK
Lingfield Point
McMullen Road
Darlington
Co. Durham
DL1 1YQ
UK
www.coatscrafts.co.uk

Rowan Yarns Ltd
Westminster Fibers, Inc.
4 Townsend West, Unit 8
Nshua, New Hampshire 03063
(603) 886 5041
(800) 445 9276
www.personalthreads.com/westminsterfibers.htm

# Index

# Acknowledgments

The publishers would like to thank the
following for their help with this book:
John Heseltine for the photography (except
for pages 50, 52 and 72 by Steven Wooster),
Anne Wilson for the design; Kate Simunek
for the artwork; and Tracey Whittington at
Coats Crafts UK for supplying yarns, threads
and equipment.